SCI v

D0500191

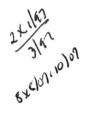

In the last century, the theory of infinite sets, created by the German mathematician Georg Cantor, has occupied one of the key positions in mathematics.

Its concepts reflect the most general properties of mathematical objects. However, in view of the discovery of a series of paradoxes in this theory, many eminent scholars doubt the soundness of its foundations.

This book is a popular account of the roads followed by human thought in attempts to understand the idea of the infinite in physics and in mathematics. It tells the reader about fundamental concepts of set theory, about its evolution, and about the relevant contributions of Russian scientists.

The book is meant for a broad range of readers who want to know how the notion of the infinite has changed in time, what one studies in set theory and what is the present state of that theory.

Editor-in-chief
A.S. Solodovnikov,
Doctor of Physical and
Mathematical Sciences.

In Search of Infinity

N. Ya. Vilenkin

Translated by Abe Shenitzer
with the editorial assistance of
Hardy Grant and Stefan Mykytiuk

Birkhäuser
Boston • Basel • Berlin

Translator
Abe Shenitzer
Department of Mathematics & Statistics
York University
North York, Ontario M3J IP3
Canada

Library of Congress Cataloging-in-Publication Data

Vilenkin, N. Ya. (Naum Yakovlevich)
[V poiskakh beskonechnosti. English]
In search of infinity / N. Ya. Vilenkin : translated by Abe
Shenitzer, with the editorial assistance of Hardy Grant and Stefan
Mykytiuk.
     p.   c.m
   Includes bibliographical references.
   ISBN 0-8176-3819-9 (H : alk. paper). -- ISBN 3-7643-3819-9 (H :
alk. paper)
   1. Infinite. 2. Set theory. I. Title.
QA9.V5513 1995   95-34319
  511.3'22--dc20   CIP

Printed on acid-free paper
© Birkhäuser Boston 1995

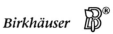 *Birkhäuser*

ISBN 0-8176-3819-9
ISBN 3-7643-3819-9
Reformatted by Texniques, Inc., Brighton, MA from translator's diskettes
Printed and bound by Quinn-Woodbine, Woodbine, NJ
Printed in the United States of America

9 8 7 6 5 4 3 2 1

Table of Contents

Introduction

The concept of infinity is one of the most important, and at the same time, one of the most mysterious concepts of science. Already in antiquity many philosophers and mathematicians pondered over its contradictory nature. In mathematics, the contradictions connected with infinity intensified after the creation, at the end of the 19th century, of the theory of infinite sets and the subsequent discovery, soon after, of paradoxes in this theory. At the time, many scientists ignored the paradoxes and used set theory extensively in their work, while others subjected set-theoretic methods in mathematics to harsh criticism. The debate intensified when a group of French mathematicians, who wrote under the pseudonym of Nicolas Bourbaki, tried to erect the whole edifice of mathematics on the single notion of a set. Some mathematicians greeted this attempt enthusiastically while others regarded it as an unnecessary formalization, an attempt to tear mathematics away from life-giving practical applications that sustain it. These differences notwithstanding, Bourbaki has had a significant influence on the evolution of mathematics in the twentieth century.

In this book we try to tell the reader how the idea of the infinite arose and developed in physics and in mathematics, how the theory of infinite sets was constructed, what paradoxes it has led to, what significant efforts have been made to eliminate the resulting contradictions, and what routes scientists are trying to find that would provide a way out of the many difficulties.

Chapter 1

Infinity and the universe

From mythology to science. The study of stone figures and of drawings, made on cave walls with ochre and charcoal, shows convincingly that tens of thousands of years ago humans not only collected information about animals and birds, about properties of grasses and fruits, but also tried to establish regularities in the world around them and to understand its origins. This is how the oldest myths arose: myths about the "Great Original Mother," the common ancestor of humans and animals, and about totems – protectors of tribes. Ancient humans attributed menacing natural phenomena – thunder, lightning, earthquakes and hurricanes – to the influence of otherworldly forces.

The development of agriculture and cattle breeding increased the importance of celestial observations. The conjunction of heavenly bodies was a signal for sowing and harvesting. From the heavens came rain that irrigated fields and pastures. The locust, one of the most formidable enemies of the ancient farmer, fell from the heavens on crops and orchards. Small wonder that ancient mythology embraced both Heaven and Earth.

Small wonder also that humans deified the forces of nature and thought that the heavens were the abode of the gods. This was the source of the first myths about the origin of the world and about the connections between natural phenomena. In almost all these myths the initial state of the world was described as either chaos or an ocean. Then came the separation of heaven and earth, and, on the earth, of water and land. Thus Akkadian myths tell of the god Marduk, who vanquished the goddess Tiamat, symbol of the primeval ocean, and fashioned heaven and earth out of her gigantic body which he split in two.

The symbolic element is more pronounced in the myths of ancient India. These myths are due to Aryan tribes that invaded Hindustan between 1500 and 1200 BC. These myths tell of the battle of the Danavs and the Adityas, of *the constrained* and *the unbounded*, or *the limited* and *the unlimited*. The triumph of the Adityas was secured by Indra, apparently the son of Heaven and Earth. When, by a miracle, he grew to frightful size, the terrified Heaven and Earth scattered in opposite directions.

Similar myths existed in ancient Iran. In the distant past the culture of the Iranians was the same as that of the Aryans. According to Iranian stories, the god Ormazd created out of sparkling metal the light and bright heaven in the form of an egg. Its top reached the Infinite World. All creatures were created in the interior of heaven. The Iranians thought that the earth was round and suspended in the center of heaven like the yoke in the center of an egg.

According to ancient Greek mythology, the world was divided into three regions – the underground kingdom, the earth, and the sky, surrounded on all sides by an ocean (this explained why water spurts upward from springs and falls to the earth as rain).

Myths enabled people to relate unconnected concepts and to make some kind of sense of the world around them. The element of action in myths was outside space and time and was not subject to the restrictions of logic. Because it reflected the experience of earlier generations, a myth could not be refuted by the argument that it contradicted the experience of an individual.

The development of manufacturing and the increased complexity of social relations were accompanied by the slow evolution of a new conceptual framework that made it possible to bypass mythology and to use logic to verify the consistency of deductions. Myths began to contradict reason and logical criteria, fewer of them were created, and the beginnings of science appeared.

Tradition links the beginning of the scientific mindset to the Greek philosopher Thales[1] who predicted the solar eclipse of 585 BC. This prediction could not have been made at a time when the sun and moon were thought of as the eyes of Heaven or as the gods Helios and Selene.

Basing himself on the Indo-Iranian idea of the contest between the bounded and the infinite, Anaximander[2] developed the doctrine that the universe derives from the infinite – the *apeiron* – which is inexhaustible and eternal. He taught that there are an infinite number of worlds that stand apart, that these worlds come into being, and when they perish they are reabsorbed into the infinite.

Much in the doctrines of Thales, Anaximander and their students strikes us now as naive (for example, Thales' notion than humans derive from fish). But these doctrines also included brilliant guesses, such as the spherical shape of the earth, the evolution of living creatures, and many others.

From the viewpoint of this book, what is most important in the doctrines of these philosophers is that they initiated the discussion of limitlessness and of infinity, and that they clarified the question of the finite or infinite nature of the universe. To clarify the idea of unboundedness, Anaximander said that "wherever the warrior stands he can extend his spear farther." This idea was later repeated by Archytas, an eminent mathematician of the Pythagorean school who lived in the fourth century BC. Democritus, the famous atomist of antiquity, thought that the universe is not only infinite but also centerless. In the first century BC, this thought was expounded in verse form by the Roman poet and philosopher Titus Lucretius Carus:

> It has no bounds, no end, no limit,
> And it matters not what part of the universe you are in;
> Wherever you are, from the spot you take up,
> It stretches to infinity in all directions.

A few centuries later, Nizami, the great poet of Central Asia, asked:

> Is there direction in the infinite world?
> Can endless distances be measured?

Thus the idea of the infinite arose in the East, reached the Greek philosophers and scholars who studied it, and returned to the East. The eminent German mathematician Hermann Weyl[3] wrote that the intuition of the infinite, and its calm and unquestioned acknowledgment, were present in the Eastern world, but there this intuition remained an abstract awareness. According to Weyl, the great achievement of Greek science was the transformation of the polar opposition between the finite and the infinite into a prolific tool for acquiring knowledge of reality.

We note that the idea of the eternity of the universe also originated in the East, as indicated by the following ancient Eastern parable: "There is a diamond mountain a thousand cubits tall. Once in a hundred years a bird comes flying and gnaws the mountain with its beak. When it has gnawed away the whole mountain, the first instant of eternity will have passed."[*]

The ancient Greek philosopher Heraclitus very clearly expressed the idea that the world is eternal and that it changes in time. He taught that " all things flow, and it is not possible to step into the same river twice, for he who does will be washed by other waters." He also said that "this cosmos was made

---

[*]In other variants of this parable the mountain is ground down by the fairy Lilavati, who comes dancing once in a hundred years and touches the mountain with the end of her train.

by neither god nor man, but always was, and is, and will be: ever-living fire, kindling in measures and quenching in measures."

Heraclitus' cosmology is very far removed from the myths of antiquity. Indeed, a study of ancient myths shows that space and time were once thought to be finite, discontinuous, and made up of qualitatively different pieces. Then the idea of evolution of the world was foreign to the human mind, and time seemed to flow in a circular manner, with constant repetition of the seasons and of the positions of the planets and stars. (It is no accident that in ancient Greek mythology Chronos, the god of time, is the son of Uranus, the god of Heaven, and philologists find that the words *time* and *rotation* have a common origin.) And even when men began to think of time as flowing in one direction, they assumed that the world had a beginning (*creation of the world*) and would end (the *last judgment* of the Gospels, the *twilight of the gods* in Scandinavian mythology, and so on). Space seemed bounded by the heavenly firmament that was the abode of the gods. It took a truly revolutionary change of human consciousness for the notion of a boundless world to emerge, a world without beginning or end. (As we shall see below this notion struck many of the best minds in the ancient world as rather bold.)

Like grains of sand at the seashore. In antiquity, philosophy, science, and mathematics were so closely related that, as a rule, all three were pursued by the same people. For example, Thales not only philosophized about the limitless and predicted eclipses but also proved, for the first time, geometric theorems. Again, tradition credits Pythagoras, founder of an influential philosophical school in the sixth century BC, with the discovery of the famous theorem about a right triangle.

Pythagoras claimed that "all is number," and some numbers (1,4,7,10) played a special role in his world view. Incidentally, the number 7 played a special role for the ancient Sumerians, long before mathematics began to develop in Greece. In their myths there are seven storm spirits, seven nasty diseases, seven regions of the underworld locked with seven doors, and so on. Again, seven celestial bodies move across the firmament. An unknown Greek philosopher, a contemporary of Thales and Anaximander, claimed that the external form of things as well as their essence must reflect the number seven; in particular, he listed seven spheres of the universe (the sphere of pure zephyr, the stars, the sun, the moon, of air, water, and earth). Some scholars think that the mystical role of the number seven goes back to the time when people counted to six and seven stood for *many* (even today we use the expressions "seven don't wait for one," "measure seven times, cut once," and so on).

Neither the Greek nor the Egyptian scholars could express very large numbers. That was because they were unaware of the idea of positional notation. The Babylonians, who knew positional notation, had too utilitarian an approach to mathematics to consider such impractical questions as, say, the number of grains of sand at the seashore. It is interesting that according to the ancient Greek "Texts of the pyramids" the ferryman of the underworld tests the soul of a dead king to see if he can count to ten. The dead soul's answer takes the form of a poem in which the ten fingers are listed in their order. This is undoubtedly an echo of a time when finger counting bordered on magic.

And even when people learned to express by means of numbers the quantity of warriors in an army or the quantity of loaves of bread needed to feed the slaves who built colossal temples and pyramids, they had no knowledge of numbers now called billion, trillion, quadrillion, and so on. To describe large numbers they resorted to comparisons: "as much as there is sand and dust," "as much as there is sand at the seashore," "like the weight of a mountain balanced by weights," "like the number of leaves on trees." At that time, even the best scientists couldn't tell which was larger: the number of grains of sand at the seashore or of leaves in the forest.

In the third century BC, some 250 years after the Greek philosophers began to discuss the concept of boundlessness, Archimedes created a system for designating very large numbers. In his "Sand-reckoner" he created a calculus for designating numbers up to $10^{8 \cdot 10^{16}}$. How large this number is can be surmised by noting that 10^{150} neutrons suffice to fill all of our metagalaxy (that is, the universe). Again, if one used decimal notation and wrote 400 digits on a meter-long strip of paper, then the strip of paper needed to record Archimedes' number would be so long that it would take a ray of light about eight days to traverse it.

Large though it is, Archimedes' number is finite. One can't write down the infinite sequence of natural numbers on a strip of paper so long that it can be wound into a ball the size of our galaxy, or into $10^{8 \cdot 10^{16}}$ such balls.

The ancient Hindus were also fascinated by large numbers. Some Hindu stories tell of battles that involved 10^{23} monkeys, and of tests in the course of which Buddha named enormous numbers. No matter that the whole solar system could not accommodate 10^{23} monkeys. Such number games were incarnations of the notion of infinity and they bewitched Greeks and Hindus alike. Archimedes and the Hindus were delighted with the thought of creating a symbolic calculus that made it possible to express such huge numbers on a small wax tablet or a strip of papyrus, thus going beyond visual contemplation.

A mysterious paradox. The idea of the infinite in science came from various sources. The questions: Is the universe bounded? Did it have a beginning? Will it have an an end? were one such source. One of the most vital questions that ancient Greek philosophers contended with was the structure of the world in the small. Daily experience showed that a loaf of bread could be shared by two, three, or at most ten people, and it could be broken into some ten thousand crumbs. Could the loaf of bread be further subdivided? And is there a limit to divisibility of material objects? Experience alone could not supply an answer to this question, and so the question of the limits of divisibility of objects shifted from the realm of experience to that of speculation.

Some philosophers maintained that matter is infinitely divisible. Thus Anaxagoras claimed that "there is no least among small things; there is always something smaller. For that which exists cannot cease to exist as a result of division regardless of how far the latter continues." He thought that the continuous cannot consist of discrete elements "separated from one another, as if split from one another by the blows of an axe." Anaxagoras and his followers seemed to think of a set of discrete points in terms of a heap of dust and of a continuum in terms of a bronze or iron sword.

The other school derived from the Pythagoreans. Its followers assumed that there exist smallest particles of matter, *atoms*, whose hardness makes them indivisible (in Greek "atom" means indivisible). These ideas were developed by Leucippus[4] and Democritus. Atomists also introduced the notion of indivisible and dimensionless parts of space (*amers*). Some scholars claim that these ideas go back to Democritus while others ascribe them to Epicurus.[5] It is difficult to decide who is right, because all that has come down to us from Democritus' many works are meagre fragments.

The conflict between the two philosophical schools was exacerbated when, in the middle of the 5th century BC, the Greek philosopher Zeno of Elea[6] showed the paradoxical consequences of careless use of the assumption of the unlimited divisibility of space and time. The best known of Zeno's paradoxes are the *Dichotomy* and the *Achilles*. In the *Dichotomy* Zeno shows that a moving object is at rest. After all, argued Zeno, before it reaches its aim the object must cover half the distance involved, and before that a quarter, and before that an eighth, and so on. Since space is infinitely divisible, the process of halving will never end. In the *Achilles*, Zeno shows in a similar manner that the fleetfooted Achilles, who covers ten stadia in a minute, will never catch up with the slow tortoise who covers one stadium in a minute.

Of course, Zeno's arguments about the impossibility of motion in the real world are contradicted by everyday experience. When the famous philosopher-cynic Diogenes[7] learned about Zeno's arguments he simply got up and walked.[*] But Zeno's arguments showed that the views on infinity in contemporary mathematics were extremely naive. In particular, Zeno was the first to show that a segment can be decomposed into infinitely many parts each of which has nonzero length. If we replaced his geometric segment by a finite time interval then we could prove the paradoxical conclusion that we could name all of the infinitely many natural numbers in an hour's time. To do this we would name the first natural number in the first half hour, the second in the next quarter hour, the third in the next eighth of an hour, and so on. We could thus fit the infinite in the finite – the infinite sequence of natural numbers in a finite time interval.

This attempt cannot be realized; the number 100, say, would have to be uttered in 2^{-100} hours – a time interval far shorter than the fastest process known to modern science. Another barrier to such speed is that no information can be transmitted with speed greater than the speed of light. Also, when one attempts to subdivide space into smaller and smaller parts one comes up against its quantum properties. But these are considerations that pertain to the real world, whereas (to use modern parlance) Zeno investigated one of its mathematical models that admits unlimited halving of space and time intervals. For this model objections of physicists are irrelevant.

Over the centuries, judgments concerning Zeno's paradoxes have changed many times. Just when it seemed that they had been completely refuted, a careful analysis would show that, whatever the level of knowledge, there remained something unexplained – a germ of new contradictions, of new knowledge. A. Fraenkel,[8] the eminent specialist in the area of infinite sets and the foundations of mathematics, put it thus:

> The bridging of the chasm between the domains of the discrete and the continuous, or between arithmetic and geometry, is one of the most important – nay, the most important – problem of the foundations of mathematics.... Of course, the character of reasoning has changed, but, as always, the difficulties are due to the chasm between the discrete and the continuous – that permanent stumbling block which also plays an extremely important role in mathematics, philosophy, and even physics.

---

[*]Of course, Diogenes' reaction had everything to do with Zeno's conclusion and nothing to do with his arguments.(Translator).

Later we will learn of other paradoxes associated with the notion of infinity that may make Zeno's paradoxes look quite naive. But the eminent Russian philosopher G.I. Naan[9] observed that mankind will never be able to completely refute the Eleatic philosopher because the infinite is inexhaustible, and Zeno managed to capture in naive but brilliant form three *eternal* problems that are very close to one another and to the problem of infinity, namely the problem of nothing, the problem of continuity, and the problem of existence. It was no accident that Aristotle called Zeno "the founder of dialectic," and Hegel regarded him as the father of dialectic in the modern sense of the word.

As could be expected, there were attempts to use Zeno's paradoxes to bolster idealism. As one famous German idealist philosopher put it, in Zeno's paradoxes infinity plays the role of a dissolvent of reality.

We won't go into further details of the role of Zeno's paradoxes in physics and philosophy. Their role in mathematics was that they uncovered the conflict between the discrete and the continuous and showed the danger of thoughtless use of the infinite. After Zeno one could not, like the sophist Antiphon,[10] regard a circle as a polygon with infinitely many sides and in this way compute its area. This was the beginning of the period of elimination of the infinite from mathematics.

A desperate attempt to do without infinite processes in geometry was due to Democritus. He tried to base geometry on his atomic doctrine. Had he succeeded, the form of geometry would have been very different from what it is. But long before Democritus, the discovery was made in the school of Pythagoras that the side and diagonal of a square are incommensurable. And this could not be so if the side of a square and its diagonal consisted of a finite number of indivisible parts. Also, while Democritus managed to compute the volume of a pyramid using his method, he could not decide whether or not *neighboring* cross sections of a pyramid are equal; indeed, if they are, then the pyramid could not contract to a point, and if they are not then the pyramid would not be smooth. As a result of these difficulties his textbook of geometry lost out to Euclid's famous *Elements*, based on the idea of unlimited divisibility of space. And philosophers intent on refuting Zeno's paradoxes had to look for approaches other than atomism.

On shaky ground. Aristotle, one of the greatest philosophers of antiquity, gave a great deal of thought to the notion of the infinite and its properties. When he discusses this subject in his works he warns that the topic entails walking on very shaky ground. Indeed, after Zeno and Democritus the concept of the infinite was mired in contradictions. Aristotle admitted that "much that is impossible follows from negating the existence of the infinite as well as from accepting it." He gave five reasons for believing in the existence of the infinite. Four are: the infinity of time, the infinite divisibility of magnitudes employed in mathematics, the fact that the infinite prevents the cessation of the phenomena of coming into existence and of annihilation, and the fact that the finite always abuts on something, and thus there is no limit to the finite. The fifth reason – the reason Aristotle regarded as the weightiest – was that there are no bounds to thought. Specifically, there are no bounds on numbers, or on mathematical magnitudes, or on what is beyond heaven. And if what is beyond heaven is infinite, then there are many worlds.

And yet, all these weighty arguments notwithstanding, "the Philosopher" (Aristotle's sobriquet in antiquity and (especially) later) refused to accept the idea of the existence of an infinite world, saying that in matters of the infinite one cannot trust thought.

We won't go into the subtleties of Aristotle's reasoning in which he analyzes various consequences of the assumption of the existence of the infinite.

What is most important for us is the distinction Aristotle drew between the *actual infinite* and the *potential infinite*, that is between an existing infinity and an infinity in the state of becoming. To obtain an example of each type of infinity, consider Zeno's process of unlimited halving of a segment. An example of an actual infinity is the totality of parts of a segment resulting from its *completed* subdivision by repeated halving. An example of a potential infinity is the process, evolving in time, of its continued subdivision by halving. Aristotle also introduced two other notions of infinity now known as *extensive* and *intensive*. The first arises as a result of successive and unlimited addition of new objects, and the second is the result of delving indefinitely deeper into the structure of an object under investigation.

Aristotle acknowledged the existence of only the potential infinite. He said that "The infinite does not actually exist as an infinite solid or magnitude apprehended by the senses.... The infinite exists potentially, the infinite is motion..."

Aristotle rejected Zeno's arguments by saying that what moves does so unconsciously. He also rejected the notion of an infinite universe; he thought that it was bounded by the ultimate sphere beyond which there was neither matter nor space. Unlike Plato, who thought that the world was the work of a Demiurge (creator), Aristotle claimed that it was not created and was eternal. (Aristotle's view that the world was not created earned him later the enmity of many theologians.)

After Aristotle it was acknowledged that "science is true to the extent to which it is based on the assumption that the discontinuous does not consist of the indivisible."

Mathematicians also stopped using the concept of infinity. For example, in his *Elements* Euclid doesn't use the concept of the infinite even where it would be quite natural to do so. Euclid does not say that there are infinitely many primes but that the number of primes exceeds any preassigned natural number. He moves triangles and other finite figures but never moves an infinite plane. He tries to use motions of even finite figures as little as possible – after Zeno the concept of motion became logically suspect.

To avoid the use of the infinite, Euclid's predecessor, the Greek mathematician Eudoxus,[11] formulated an axiom which, in effect, denied the existence of infinitely small and infinitely large magnitudes. It was to the effect that a suitable integral multiple of the smaller of two given magnitudes will exceed the larger one. This axiom was the basis of the *method of exhaustion* used by Euclid and Archimedes to prove theorems about areas and volumes.

Rebirth of the infinite. The last centuries of antique civilization were marked by the decline of learning and by the spread of superstitions and of beliefs in miracles and omens. There was a gradual decline of the oral tradition that enabled people to understand the complex reasoning of the great scholars of the flourishing period of that civilization. Faith in magicians, miracle workers and prophets flourished. The triumph of Christian dogma completed the process of slow death of antique philosophy and learning. In 415 AD a mob of Christian fanatics, incited by the Alexandrian bishop Cyril, lynched Hypatia,[12] one of the last representatives of ancient culture, and burned the Alexandrian library that preserved the treasures of that culture.

For many centuries after that, philosophy was reduced to the role of a servant of theology. Old superstitions that the flat Earth is supported by three whales got a new lease on life. The words of the theologian Tertullian – "It is certain because it is impossible" – became the slogan of that time. The infinite also ended up in the theological sphere – it became an attribute of God.

But slowly the ideas of Plato and Aristotle again acquired currency and the difficult job of reconciling Church dogma and the teachings of the ancient philosophers began. While the most zealous theologians rejected the teachings of the pagan philosophers, an ever larger number of scholars adopted the viewpoint of Albert the Great:[13] "I am not concerned with divine miracles when I reason about natural things using natural logic." Already in the 14th century some scholastics acknowledged the eternity of the world and the mortality of the human soul.

The controversies between theologians and philosophers gave rise to new ideas that undermined religious dogmas as well as the world view of the followers of Aristotle. In 1277 the Paris bishop Etienne Tempier attacked the teaching of the Philosopher about the eternity and the noncreatedness of the universe but, at the same time, admitted the idea of the possible plurality of worlds. He even advanced the idea that the heavenly spheres can have not only circular but also rectilinear motion. But that meant that there was space beyond the ultimate sphere! This was a first step to admitting the possibility of an infinite universe, although Tempier's teaching contains no explicit statement to this effect.

In the 14th century Thomas Bradwardine[14] arrived at the idea of the existence of a vacuum. Then there were scholastics who rejected Aristotle's thesis about the nonexistence of the actual infinite. The so-called infinitists claimed that the notion of the actual infinite contained no contradiction whatever and such an infinite could therefore exist. At the beginning of the 14th century John Baconthorpe[15] asserted that every magnitude – number, time, a collection of solids – could be actually infinite, and that a solid could be subdivided into an infinite number of parts. This undermined the foundation of Aristotelian cosmology.

The final demolition of ancient cosmology came in the 15th and 16th centuries and is linked to the names of Nicolas Cusa[16] and Giordano Bruno. Cusa developed the doctrine of the maximum, that is something that cannot be exceeded. This was one of the greatest achievements of Renaissance dialectics and prepared a revolution not only in cosmology but also in the mathematical way of thinking. Thus Cusa maintained that a line is a circle of infinite radius and considered not individual figures but the limiting states of figures resulting from various modifications of their form.

The notion of the infinite also attracted the attention of astronomers. In his great work Nicholas Copernicus maintained that the distance between the Earth and the Sun is imperceptibly small in comparison with the heavenly firmament. The sphere of stars he regarded as very similar to the infinite. He sometimes said that Heaven is immeasurably greater than the Earth and represents an infinitely large magnitude. But he left it up to other scholars to decide whether the Universe is infinite or merely immeasurably large.

The final step in the demolition of old dogmas was taken by Giordano Bruno who paid with his life for his scientific exploit. Bruno wrote:

The universe is one, infinite, immovable... It cannot be grasped and is therefore incalculable and limitless, and thus infinite and boundless, and, therefore, immovable. It does not move in space, for there is nothing outside it where it could transfer, because it is all. It is not born... for it is all existence. It is not annihilated, for there is no other thing into which it could change. It can neither decrease nor increase, for it is infinite.

This is how the human spirit was freed from the limitations that fettered it. Bruno expressed the spirit of the new era in the following verse:

I rise high and boldly break
The imaginary barrier of the crystal sphere.
I rush to infinity, to different distances.
Some are destined for grief and some for joy, –
The Milky Way I leave below for you.

Of course, many found the new world now revealed to the eye of the mind most uncomfortable. The heavenly spheres containing the orderly universe of antiquity and the Middle Ages were demolished. The world appeared before man located in nothingness, surrounded by nothingness and permeated by nothingness through and through. At the beginning of the 17th century the Paris parliament issued a decree that anyone coming out with a polemic against ancient and universally recognized authors would be subject to capital punishment. At the same time, the Holy Inquisition conducted two trials against Galileo Galilei, the greatest physicist and mathematician of the time, and, by threatening to burn him at the stake, forced him to publicly reject the ideas of Copernicus and Bruno, and sentenced him to house arrest for the rest of his life.

But times were changing. To solve practical problems scientists found it necessary to apply methods forbidden by Aristotelian science and to use indivisible and infinitely small magnitudes. There was renewed interest in the ideas of Democritus. Using "illegitimate" methods, Kepler obtained formulas for the volumes of various solids that baffled adherents of ancient rigor. He also used these methods in the immortal works in which he established the laws of motion of the planets around the Sun. Using the ideas of his teacher Galileo, the Italian mathematician Bonaventura Cavalieri[17] wrote a book titled *Geometry of indivisibles* in which he stated principles that made it possible to compute areas and volumes of various figures by means of a general method. Toward the end of the 17th century Newton and Leibniz independently systematized the methods of solution of a tremendous variety of problems, methods based on the use of infinitely small and infinitely large magnitudes. This was the genesis of mathematical analysis (differential and integral calculus), one of the most remarkable creations of the human mind. Knowing the forces acting on a body one could, by the methods of mathematical analysis, determine that body's trajectory. In particular, one could in this way determine the orbits of planets and comets.

The ideas of Copernicus, Bruno, Galileo, and Newton interested not only scientists. At the end of the 17th century, the French writer Fontenelle[18] wrote *On the multiplicity of worlds*, a work translated into many languages. And the 18th-century German poet Albert von Haller wrote:

I amass countless numbers,
I pile millions into a mountain,
I pour time in a heap,
Ranges of innumerable worlds.
When I look at you
From a reckless height,
Then I see that you are
Far above all numbers and measures:
They are just part of you.

The new ideas were propagated in Russia by Lomonosov, the poet and great founder of Russian science. He expressed his idea of the world's infinity in these inspired lines:

The chasm opened, full of stars,
The stars numberless, the chasm bottomless.

And the poet Sumarokov embedded these ideas in his translation of the biblical psalms. His rival Tred'yakovskii denounced him to the Holy Synod in these words: "While reading the September 1755 issue of 'Monthly works', I, the undersigned, found in it holy odes by Colonel Aleksandr Petrov, son of Sumarokov. Among them I found an ode based on Psalm 106, and saw that, from the eighth stanza to the eleventh inclusive, it speaks – in its own words and not those of the psalmist – of the infinity of the universe and of the actual multitude of worlds, and not about what is possible owing to divine omnipotence."

After receiving this denunciation, the Holy Fathers demanded that Czarina Elisabeth should suppress the journal which, they said, "contains much that is contrary to the holy faith, especially certain translations and works that assert the existence of many, nay, innumerable worlds, which is utterly repulsive to the Holy Writ and to Christian faith and gives weak souls reasons for naturalism and atheism."

But the eighteenth century was coming, and the czarina "took no action" on the humble request of the Holiest Synod.

Newton's world. In astronomy, physics and mathematics, the end of the 17th century witnessed the triumph of ideas connected, in one way or another, with the use of the infinite. There came into being a picture of the world ruled by Euclidean geometry and Newton's laws of motion. Scientists assumed that knowing the positions of all material bodies at a given moment they could, by solving the appropriate differential equations, predict their positions at an arbitrary future moment.

The two foundations of the whole edifice had nothing to do with one another. Infinite space was completely unrelated to the matter that filled it – it was just a stage that accommodated the drama of the world. By its very nature this space was unrelated to everything external and remained forever the same and immobile. It would not change even if all matter suddenly vanished. In this connection Einstein wrote:

> Newton found that observed geometric magnitudes (distances be-
> tween material points) and their changes in time do not, in a physi-
> cal sense, fully characterize motion. . . Thus, in addition to masses
> and to distances between points that change in time there exists
> something else that determines the occurring events; this "some-
> thing" he took to be the relation to absolute space.

As a result of the successes of Newtonian mechanics and astronomy, the world picture proposed by Newton gained universal acceptance. Doubts about it came to be regarded as antiscientific.

The famous German philosopher Kant described the picture of the universe accepted in the 18th century in these words:

> In the infinite distance there are many such systems of stars, and
> its parts are mutually related. . . . We see the first members of an
> unbroken series of worlds and systems, and the first part of this
> infinite progression gives us an idea of the whole. There is no
> end here, there is a truly immeasurable chasm. . . . The universe is
> filled with worlds without number and end. . .

It should be noted that the recognition of the infinity of the universe "co-existed peacefully" with faith in God in the mind of Kant and in the minds of most of his contemporaries. In fact, some theologians argued that it took a more powerful God to create an infinite rather than a finite world and saw in the infinity of the universe a "proof of God's omnipotence." It took half a century of the activities of Voltaire and the Encyclopedists, and the horrors of the French revolution, to make possible an intellectual climate in which Laplace could say to Napoleon who asked him why his works on celestial mechanics make no mention of God: "Your Highness, I have no need of this hypothesis."

New complications. Not in vain did Aristotle warn about the shaky and vague nature of the concept of infinity and of the complications it could lead to. The first complications in Newtonian physics and mathematical analysis arose soon after their creation.

The students and followers of Newton and Leibniz used the vague concepts of the infinitely small and infinitely large, full of mystery, to solve the most complex problems of astronomy, physics and mechanics. They proceeded recklessly. They unceremoniously added infinitely many terms without pausing to ask whether or not the rules of operation applicable to finite sums carried over to infinite sums. But while the fundamental concepts of the new calculus struck mathematicians brought up on ancient rigor as nebulous, its practical triumphs allayed for a time all doubts. D'Alembert,[19] one of the great 18th century French mathematicians, told his students "Go ahead, and faith will come."

But at the end of the 18th century came the first signs of trouble. Cases began to accumulate where incorrect application of infinitely small and infinitely large magnitudes led to paradoxes. As a result, in the beginning of the 19th century these magnitudes were banished from mathematics and replaced by the idea of limit. In this the works of Abel,[20] Cauchy,[21] and Gauss,[22] the "prince of mathematicians," played a collective role. The following excerpt from Gauss' letter to Schumacher,[23] written in 1831, is typical of his view of the infinite:

> I object to the use of an infinite magnitude as something completed; this is never admissible in mathematics. One must not interpret infinity literally when, strictly speaking, one has in mind a limit approached with arbitrary closeness by ratios as other things increase without bounds.

Another area where complications arose was cosmology. The natural assumptions about the uniform distribution of stars in infinite space led unexpectedly to a paradox. It turned out that their collective brightness would be the same as if a Sun glittered at every point in the sky. It was an image an Indian poet had in mind many centuries earlier when he exclaimed:

> The sky above would shine
> With boundless and awesome force
> If a thousand Suns at once flashed in it.

This was the so-called *photometric*, or Olbers' paradox. There was another, so-called *gravitational* paradox. It turned out that if the infinite Universe contained a finite amount of matter, then all of it would collect in one place, in a single lump. And if the total mass were infinite and uniformly distributed, then this would lead to a mutual equilibration of gravitational forces.

Both paradoxes can be eliminated by assuming that matter is distributed in the Universe nonuniformly. But this leads to the hypothesis that the Universe has a center. This is no less surprising than the notion of finiteness of mass in the Universe. Here we note that contemporary observations show that matter is more or less uniformly distributed throughout the Metagalaxy (= total physical Universe).

The photometric and gravitational paradoxes could be removed only after the introduction, in the 20th century, of a new theory of the structure of the Universe based on Einstein's general theory of relativity. Before telling you about these new notions we'll make another excursion into mathematics.

Curved space. The following passage is taken from the novel *The Astronauts*, by the science-fiction writer Stanislaw Lem:

> The picture of the starry sky changed very rapidly. Yesterday's photographs didn't match today's. It seemed that a mysterious force was pushing them apart. It was as if they were specks on the surface of a constantly expanding balloon. The gravitologist of the astral expedition was at the computer for days. The expedition was approaching a heavy star that was strongly curving the surrounding space. To determine the course of the ship this curvature had to be constantly computed. This was a crucial check. Humans were encountering such strong gravitational fields, such large space curvatures, for the first time. Einstein's equations were now being put to a test. The success of the expedition, and even the lives of its members, depended on them.

What is most baffling in this passage to a reader unfamiliar with modern mathematics is the reference to the curvature of space. It is much more difficult to imagine curved space than a curved line or surface. Small wonder that the creation of the concept of curved space in the second half of the 19th century inspired the (German) epigram:

Die Menschen fassen kaum es
Das Krümmungsmass des Raumes

(people seem unable to grasp what is [meant by] the measure of curvature of space).

The common objections to the notion of curved space are these: A curved line cannot be brought into coincidence with a straight line; it can be disposed in a plane or in space. Similarly, a curved surface can't be disposed in a plane – this requires at least three-dimensional space. Thus curved space must lie in some ambient space of four, or perhaps five, dimensions. And since no one has observed four-dimensional space, the space we live in can't possibly be curved. Incidentally, the notion of four-dimensional space is a favorite of science-fiction writers. In many of H.G. Wells' stories voyages take place in the fourth dimension.

It turns out that curvature of space has nothing to do with the fourth dimension and is, so to say, one of its intrinsic aspects. In fact, the curvature of space can be determined without leaving it, by just carrying out measurements in it.

To clarify how this is done we first explain how to find the curvature of a surface without leaving it, just by measuring distances between its points.

Geometry on planet Eks. For millennia people thought that the Earth was flat. But observations of the shadow of the Earth during lunar eclipses suggested to the ancient Greek scientists that the Earth was spherical; in fact, Eratosthenes managed to compute its radius with considerable accuracy. For a time, the idea of the flatness of the Earth reasserted itself, and it took Magellan's circumnavigation of the world to establish the spherical shape of the Earth.

And now imagine planet Eks whose sky is permanently shrouded in clouds and whose oceans are not navigable. It is inhabited by creatures capable of rational thought. Can they decide whether they live on a flat piece of land surrounded by water or on a spherical planet? In earthly terms, the question is: Could the spherical shape of the Earth have been established without Magellan's voyage? Here we are not questioning the geographical or historical significance of his voyage. Ours is a purely mathematical concern, namely the possibility of establishing the curvature of the Earth without circumnavigating it.

To understand how the idea of the curvature of a surface arises, we trace the evolution of geometry on the planet Eks.

Geometry begins as an experimental endeavor. It becomes a full-fledged science as a result of a theoretical generalization of centuries of observation pertaining to properties of space. Since the sky of planet Eks is permanently obscured by clouds, its geometers were restricted to making measurements on its surface. It turned out that among all the lines joining two points there is always a shortest one (see Figure 1). These shortest lines were called "straight-line segments."

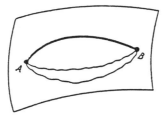

Figure 1.

Of course, an "outside" observer would say that these lines are curved rather than straight, that they are arcs of sections of a sphere by means of diametrical planes. But Ekslings couldn't look at their planet from the outside, and called the shortest curves on the surface straight lines. (It is worth pointing out that we often say that "the road is as straight as an arrow" when, in fact, it is an arc of a diametrical section.)

Next the Ekslings established various properties of these "straight lines." At first they could perform only local measurements, with poor precision. As a result, they concluded that the properties of "straight lines" on the surface of their planet were the same as the properties of straight lines in the plane. In particular, they thought that two points determine a unique "straight line" and that two "straight lines" intersect in just one point (the diametrically opposite second point of intersection was inaccessible to the observers). Finally, the Eksling geometers concluded that their "straight lines" are infinitely long. The very idea that if they moved along a "straight line" in the same direction they would eventually return to the starting point struck them as absurd, inconceivable, and contrary to common sense. They also concluded that the surface of their planet is infinite, and accused opponents of this idea of being guilty of mortal sin.

Further study of the properties of "straight lines" showed that, within the limits of available precision of measurement, the sum of the angles of a triangle was equal to 180°, that the square of the hypotenuse of a right triangle was equal to the sum of the squares of its shorter sides, and so on. In other words, the Ekslings constructed Euclidean geometry and were certain that it was applicable to the surface of their planet.

In time, the Ekslings developed their technology and could survey ever larger pieces of their planet's land (we recall that their oceans were not navigable). These more global measurements contradicted Euclidean geometry. To understand what was at issue, take three points A, B, C on a sphere as in Figure 2a. Connect them by Eksling "straight lines," or, in our parlance, by arcs of meridians AB and AC and the equatorial arc BC. The angles of the triangle ABC are all right angles, and so their sum is 270° and not, as in Euclidean geometry, 180°. It is "too large" by 90°.

Call the difference $(\alpha + \beta + \gamma) - 180°$ between the sum of the angles α, β, γ of a spherical triangle and 180° its *angular excess*. (The notion of angular excess retains its significance on an arbitrary surface.) Then the angular excess of our triangle is 90°. Other triangles have different angular excesses. Thus in the triangle ABD in Figure 2b the angles B and D are 90° each and the angle BAD is 180° so that the angular excess of triangle ABD is 180°.

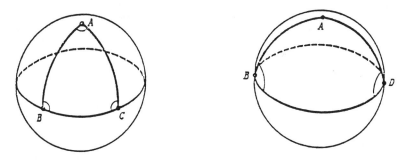

Figure 2a.   Figure 2b.

Parallel transport. The nonzero angular excess of triangles was not the only thing that persuaded Ekslings that they lived on a curved surface. Pythagoras' theorem also failed. The triangle in Figure 2a is at the same time a right triangle and an equilateral triangle!

The study of parallel straight lines on the surface of the planet (which they defined as straight lines perpendicular to one and the same straight line) also led Ekslings to unexpected results. If a segment is transported along a closed *plane* curve parallel to itself, then it will return to its initial position without change of direction (see Figure 3a). The Ekslings verified this in the small. But measurements in the large on the surface of Eks led to altogether different results.

For example, consider the triangle ABC in Figure 3b. This triangle has three right angles. We draw at A a "segment" perpendicular to AB and transport it, parallel to itself, along the contour of triangle ABC. When we reach B, the direction of our segment is the same as that of the equator. Since the equator is also a "straight line," parallel transport of our segment along BC yields a segment at C that is again directed along the equator. When this segment is parallel-transported along the meridian CA, then we obtain at A a segment rotated relative to the initial segment at A through $90°$. Again, parallel transport of a segment along the contour of $\triangle ABD$ in Figure 2b rotates it through $180°$. Note that in both cases the transported segment is rotated through an angle equal to the angular excess of the relevant triangle. This turns out to be true for *all* triangles!

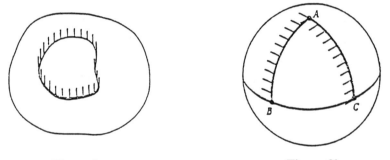

Figure 3a.   Figure 3b.

An interesting case of parallel transport is that of parallel transport of a segment around the equator (see Figure 4). At first one is inclined to think that the segment returns to its initial position without any rotation. But this is not so. Actually, the segment is rotated through $360°$. To see this supplement the equator with an arc AB of a meridian traversed in both directions. In this way we obtain a "triangle" ABA two of whose angles are $90°$ each and the third is $360°$. The angular excess of this triangle is $360°$. (To understand this case of parallel transport, it may be helpful to think of "triangle" ABA as the union of two triangles like the one in Figure 2b. (Transl.))

Measurement of curvature. We repeat: By measuring the angle sum of triangles, by noting the rotation of a segment under parallel transport along a closed contour, and by trying to verify Pythagoras' theorem, the inhabitants of planet Eks concluded that they lived not on a plane but on a curved surface. As a measure of curvature of a piece of this surface, they took the angle of rotation of a segment under parallel translation along its boundary. This curvature could also be computed by subdividing the piece of surface in question into triangles and adding their angular excesses. (This approach is justified by noting that the angular excess of a triangle that is the union of two triangles is the sum of their angular excesses.)

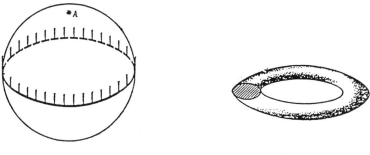

Figure 4.   Figure 5.

It turned out that the larger the area of the piece of surface the greater its curvature. Specifically, the angular excess of a triangle with area S and angles with radian measures α, β, and γ is

$$\alpha + \beta + \gamma - \pi = kS. \tag{1}$$

This showed that the curvature per unit area was constant. The Ekslings took k as a measure of curvature of the surface of their planet.

Among all surfaces there is just one for which the angular excess of a triangle per unit area is constant. This surface is a sphere. And so the Eksling geometers realized that they lived on a sphere and not on a plane. They computed its radius with relative ease. Note that the number k does not depend on the choice of triangle. Take, say, the triangle ABC in Figure 2a. The radian measure of its angular excess is $\pi/2$. Its area is one eighth of the area of a sphere of radius R, that is $\pi R^2/2$. Hence (1) reduces in this case to the equality $\pi/2 = k \cdot \frac{\pi R^2}{2}$, so that $k = 1/R^2$. It follows that for an arbitrary spherical triangle with angles α, β, γ and area S we have

$$\alpha + \beta + \gamma - \pi = S/R^2,$$

where R is the radius of the sphere. This formula allows us to compute the radius of the sphere by measuring the angles and area of a triangle on that sphere. Of course, this is not the most convenient way of computing the radius of a sphere, for it calls for accurate measurements of the angles and area of a triangle on that sphere. To compute the radius of the Earth, one computed the length of an arc of a meridian by making certain observations of the stars.

Gaussian curvature. We saw that the curvature k of a sphere per unit area is $1/R^2$. Thus the larger its radius the smaller the curvature of a piece of its surface of unit area; the surface of a ball is far more curved than the surface of the Earth.

Gauss proposed a similar measure of the curvature of an arbitrary surface. On any surface we can construct a geometry in a manner similar to the construction of spherical geometry. The role of rectilinear segments is played by the *shortest curves*, or *geodesics*, that is curves whose length is shorter than the lengths of all other curves connecting two given points. The first to encounter these curves were surveyors. Incidentally, Gauss' interest in the geometry of surfaces was the result of his involvement with a geodesic survey of the kingdom of Hannover that lasted several years.

One can construct geodesic triangles, quadrangles, and so on. Just as on a sphere, the angle sum of a (geodesic) triangle on an arbitrary curved surface is, in general, different from π. As on a sphere, we define the curvature of a triangle per unit area as $(\alpha + \beta + \gamma - \pi)/S$. On non-spherical surfaces this number can be different for different triangles; in fact, it can be positive for some triangles and negative for others.

To compute the curvature of a surface at a point, we compute the number $(\alpha + \beta + \gamma - \pi)/S$ for a sequence of ever smaller triangles around this point and seek its limit. This is Gauss' definition of the curvature of a surface at a point; hence the term *Gaussian curvature*. It is positive if the triangles involved have angle sums greater than π and negative if these sums are less than π.

The Gaussian curvature of a convex surface is everywhere positive. The Gaussian curvature of a *torus* (see Figure 5) is positive at some points and negative at others.

A remarkable property of Gaussian curvature is that it is unchanged by bending the surface, that is by subjecting it to transformations that don't change distances between points. (Such transformations are called isometries.) It follows that the Gaussian curvature of a cylinder is zero at all points; after all, a cylinder is the result of bending a piece of a plane, and the Gaussian curvature of the latter is zero everywhere. Similarly, the Gaussian curvature of a cone is zero at all of its points other than the vertex.

The pseudosphere and hyperbolic geometry. The Gaussian curvature of a sphere is constant and positive at all of its points. It is interesting that there is a surface of constant negative Gaussian curvature. This surface is called a *pseudosphere* and is obtained in the following manner.

Consider Figure 6. Imagine a person at A with a dog on a taut leash at O. The dog runs at constant speed along the straight line Ox and its owner runs after it so that her velocity is always directed along the (taut) leash. (This means that the owner is initially running in the direction AO.) As the dog continues to run along the straight line Ox, the angle between that line and the direction of the owner's velocity continues to decrease, while the distance between dog and owner stays constant. The curve traversed by the owner is called a *tractrix* and has the following property: Draw a tangent to the tractrix at a point M. If the tangent at M intersects Ox at N, then the length of the segment MN is constant. (This is clear if we bear in mind that MN represents the taut leash.)

If we reflect the tractrix in Figure 6 in the straight line OA and rotate the resulting curve about the Ox-axis, then we obtain the surface of revolution represented in Figure 7. This surface is the promised pseudosphere. As noted, its Gaussian curvature is constant and negative at all points (other than the points of the circle generated by the point A in Figure 6). What is remarkable about this surface is that its geometry is the same as that of a part of the hyperbolic plane. Thus the discovery of the pseudosphere was an important event in the evolution of non-Euclidean geometry.

Gauss and Riemann. Gauss gave a precise definition of the notion of curvature of a surface. Next on the agenda was the problem of defining the curvature of space. This problem was solved by Bernhard Riemann,[24] one of the most remarkable mathematicians of the 19th century.

Riemann dealt with the problem of curvature of space in his inaugural lecture of 1854. At that time, the (laudable) custom was that a beginning instructor was expected to present a lecture before the members of the faculty who would then be in a position to judge his teaching abilities. Riemann offered a few topics for such a lecture and Gauss selected the one that interested him most – "On the hypotheses which lie at the foundations of geometry." It is safe to assume that the listeners were not greatly impressed by Riemann's pedagogical talent. The only listener who completely understood Riemann's lecture was Gauss.

Using virtually no formulas and computations, Riemann developed general ideas on multidimensional manifolds, on measuring length on such manifolds, on their curvature, and so on. In this lecture Riemann posed questions that continue to interest theoretical physicists to this day, namely, whether our space is continuous or discrete, and whether Euclidean geometry is applicable to infinitesimal regions of space. The profundity of Riemann's ideas fascinated Gauss, and, according to some members of the audience, he went home sunk in deep thought.

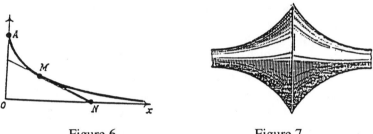

Figure 6.   Figure 7.

Curvature of a space. What was Riemann's notion of curvature of a space and how was it to be measured? Riemann used the same idea that Gauss had used for measuring the curvature of a surface, that is, he computed the angle sum of a geodesic triangle and the amount by which it differed from π. But here the difficulty is that there are many planes passing through a point in a space, and therefore many relevant triangles. Hence Riemann spoke not about curvature at a point but about curvature at a point in the direction of a given plane.

If for all triangles in a space the angle sum is π, then in this space Euclidean geometry is valid. Such a space has zero curvature and is said to be *flat*. If there are triangles with angle sum greater than π, then the curvature of the space at the relevant points is positive. Finally, if there are triangles with angle sum less than π, then the curvature of the space at the relevant points is negative. This shows that there is nothing mysterious about the notion of curvature of a space. What counts is the possibility that the angle sum of a triangle can deviate from the prescribed Euclidean value.

Spaces that have the same curvature at all points and in all planes are of great interest (they are known as *constant-curvature spaces*). In such spaces bodies can move from place to place without changing their dimensions. If the curvature of a space varies, then the dimensions of a moving body are subject to change – the body is distorted.

Riemann posed the question of the curvature of the space we live in. He wrote:

Either the actual things forming the groundwork of a space must constitute a discrete manifold, or else the basis of metric relations must be sought outside that actuality, in binding forces that operate upon it.

A decision on these questions can be found only by starting from the structure of phenomena that has been approved in experience hitherto, for which Newton laid the foundation, and by modifying this structure gradually under the compulsion of facts which it cannot explain. . .

This path leads into the domain of another science, into the realm of physics, into which the nature of this present occasion forbids us to penetrate.

The pursuit of curvature. Riemann's prediction began to be realized only at the beginning of the 20th century. It was then that the question of the curvature of space moved from the domain of abstract mathematical considerations to that of concrete physical theories. The great physicist Albert Einstein pondered the reason for the equality of inertial and gravitational masses and eventually created the general theory of relativity that radically changed our notions of the relation between matter and space. Whereas, as noted earlier, in Newton's physics space was completely independent of the matter in it, the new theory ruled out the very existence of empty, that is field-free, space. Also, it turned out that space and time cannot exist independently, but only in a state of inseparable connection with one another, and only as a structural property of a field.

Einstein's theory was so complex and unusual that many scientists reacted to it with disbelief (and many failed to understand it). An additional difficulty was that Einstein had no experimental proofs of his theory other than the equality of the two forms of mass, and physicists acknowledge a new theory only if, in addition to explaining all relevant known phenomena, it predicts new, as yet unobserved ones.

Among the many unexpected, and at first sight paradoxical, consequences of general relativity, there is one that lends itself relatively easily to experimental verification. The theory implies that attracting masses will curve space. Thus one had to give an experimental proof of the curvature of space.

A long time ago it was established by means of physical experiments that light follows a path that minimizes time, and that the speed of light in empty space is always the same. Therefore (the paths of) light rays (in empty space) are taken as geodesics in space.

To determine the curvature of space it was necessary to measure the angle sum of a triangle made up of light rays. But even in the case of triangles with a star as one vertex, the angle sum is, within experimental error, equal to π, so that the curvature of space, if any, is very small. Incidentally, unsuccessful attempts to prove the non-Euclidean nature of ordinary space by direct measurement of the angle sum of cosmic triangles go back to Lobachevski.[25]

Einstein suggested that rather than determine the angle sum of cosmic triangles one should observe changes in paths of light rays. His theory implied that if one photographed a star twice – once when a beam of its light passes far from the Sun and a second time when it passes close to the Sun, then one would notice a shift in the star's position due to the bending of the light beam.

Classical physics also predicts such an effect, but Einstein's theory predicted an effect that was double that predicted by the classical theory. Even this "large" effect is very small; in fact, it is less than two seconds of arc (the angle subtended by a two-kopeck coin at a distance of 1200 meters). Nevertheless, the effect is measurable. And while sunlight "drowns out" stars in the Sun's vicinity, the necessary observations can be carried out during a total eclipse of the Sun.

Accordingly, in the spring of 1919 two scientific expeditions were dispatched to measure the curvature of space, one to the southern shore of Africa, and the other to northern Brazil. Observations carried out by the expeditions on 29 May 1919 fully confirmed Einstein's prediction: the actual star shift was equal to that predicted by Einstein's theory.

Another proof of the curvature of space was derived from observations of Mercury. This planet is closest to the Sun and so is most affected by the curvature of the space around the Sun. As a result of this curvature, the orbit of Mercury rotates slightly with each rotation of the planet around the Sun. The orbit also rotates because of planetary attraction. But the observed rotation of the orbit of Mercury exceeded by 41 seconds of arc per 100 years the rotation due to planetary attraction alone. Based on Einstein's formulas, the computation of the rotation of the orbit of Mercury due to the curvature of space yielded the figure of 41 seconds of arc per 100 years. This result explained a riddle that had been troubling astronomers for many years and supplied a new confirmation of the theory of relativity.

The expanding Universe. Relativity theory confronted astronomers with the fundamental question of the structure of actual space. If it is curved and its curvature is positive, then it could very well be like a three-dimensional sphere – that is, unbounded but finite in size. Some philosophers rejected the very possibility of the finite size of actual space. But their arguments carried as much conviction as the arguments of Eksling scientists who thought that they lived on an infinite plane and not on a sphere of finite size. The answer to the question of the structure of actual space called for astronomical observations and not for mere speculation. The first attempt to construct a model of the Universe on the basis of the new theory of gravitation was by Einstein himself, but it was not very successful. Einstein tried to construct a model of a stationary Universe that did not change in time. It seemed to echo the words of Aristotle, who wrote that "throughout time, according to the chronicles passed on from generation to generation, we find no trace of changes either in the distant sky as a whole or in any of its accessible parts."

To construct a stationary model of the Universe, Einstein had to assume the existence of forces that repel galaxies from one another and are proportional to the distance between them. At that time, there were no known experiments that confirmed the existence of such forces. Later Einstein described the assumption of the existence of such forces of repulsion as the "biggest mistake of my life."

An unexpected solution was proposed in 1922 by the young Leningrad mathematician Aleksandr Aleksandrovich Friedmann.[26] In a paper "On the curvature of space" Friedmann showed that the equations of general relativity have nonstationary solutions – that is, solutions that imply that the Universe expands or contracts. In the first case the curvature and density of matter decrease, and in the second case both increase. It is interesting that Friedmann's major works deal with dynamical meteorology and not with theoretical physics.

Friedmann's solution was so different from established views of the structure of the Universe that the first reaction of the scientific community was to assume that he had made a mistake. This was also the tenor of a short note by Einstein that appeared in 1922 in the same journal that had published Friedmann's paper. Soon Einstein received from Friedmann a detailed letter that dispelled all his doubts. And while Einstein was at the time universally recognized as the leading physicist and Friedmann was just a beginning researcher, the venerable scientist did not hesitate for a moment how to respond. On 13 May 1923 the editor of the *Journal of Physics* (Zeitschrift für Physik) obtained a letter from Einstein which he subsequently published under the title "A note on A. Friedmann's paper on the curvature of space." The letter read:

> In a previous note I criticized the paper mentioned in the title of this note. But Friedmann's letter convinced me that my criticism was based on computational errors.
> I regard Friedmann's results as correct and as shedding new light.
> It turns out that the field equations admit not only static but also

dynamic (that is varying with time) centrally-symmetric solutions
for the structure of space.

Later it turned out that there are no static solutions. Einstein's model was
unstable, and so a homogeneous and isotropic (the same in all directions) model
of the Universe must be dynamic. Following Friedmann, many physicists and
astronomers – Lemaître,[27] de Sitter,[28] and others – constructed dynamic models
of the Universe.

The question of an experimental confirmation of the validity of one or another model of the Universe arose once more; in particular, the question to
be decided was whether the Universe expands or contracts. Then astronomers
recalled that already at the beginning of the 20th century the American astrophysicist V.M. Slipher[29] had measured the radial velocities of galaxies. It
turned out that 36 of the 41 galaxies investigated by Slipher recede from us,
and some of them do so at speeds of 2000km/sec (later it turned out that the
remaining 5 galaxies approach us because of the actual motion of the Sun in
our Galaxy). Slipher's investigations were continued by E.P. Hubble,[30] who
determined not only the velocities of galaxies but also their distances from the
Sun. His investigations established the following remarkable law: the speed
with which a galaxy recedes from us is proportional to its distance. In other
words, the most distant galaxies recede from us fastest.

This was a conclusive proof of Friedmann's guess. The Universe is expanding. This is not to say that the Earth is the center from which galaxies recede
in all directions. What it does mean is that every observer will see the same
picture – galaxies receding in all directions from the spot she occupies.

The picture of the expanding Universe made possible an explanation of the
gravitational and photometric paradoxes. It turned out that light from distant
stars does not reach the Earth, that we can only see galaxies that are closer than
the so-called *visible horizon*. As for the possibility of a contracting Universe,
we note that during such periods, if any, the photometric paradox would set in
with a vengeance, and the flood of energy engulfing the Earth would make life
impossible. In other words, life is possible during periods of expansion of the
Universe but impossible during periods of its contraction.

The past and future of the Universe. After the appearance of dynamic models
of the Universe there arose a number of questions now pondered by theoretical
physicists: When did the scattering of the galaxies begin and what preceded it?
Will the scattering persist forever or will there be a period of contraction? and
so on. Today most scientists agree that many billions of years ago the Universe

was in a superdense state. It appears that the density of this clot was greater than the density of matter in atomic nuclei – that is, greater than 10^{14}g/cm^3. Some computations give densities of the order of 10^{93}g/cm^3. One thing is clear, namely that matter was in a state completely unknown to today's physicists, and that neither gravitational laws nor quantum theory were applicable to it.

On the basis of observations of the Universe in its present state, theoretical physicists try to arrive at its state shortly after the "big bang" with which, they think, its history began. They compute when the elementary particles began to form, when these particles began to coalesce into atoms, how the temperature of the Universe began to change. In particular, these investigations have shown that if the Universe was originally "hot," then we must still be receiving today a form of electromagnetic radiation called cosmic background radiation. Different variants of the theory have assigned to this radiation temperatures as low as a fraction of one degree on the Kelvin scale and as high as 20-30 degrees on that scale.

In 1964 two Soviet theoreticians, A.G. Doroshkevich[31] and I.D. Novikov,[32] computed by how much cosmic background radiation exceeds the intensity of other sources of radiation in the centimeter range of the spectrum. But their paper, pointing out the possibility of a decisive experiment, was somehow overlooked. Cosmic background radiation was accidentally discovered (by Americans) in 1965 in the course of work with an antenna for tracking satellites. Its temperature turned out to be 3 degrees Kelvin. This discovery greatly increases the probability of the model of a hot initial state of the Universe.

We won't try to give a detailed account, based on modern views, of the creation and evolution of stars and galaxies. In this area there are many contentious points. Of all these theories (including the "big bang") the eminent physicist L.N. Brillouin[33] said that "all this is too beautiful to be true and too unlikely to be believed." Nevertheless, modern science has no other theory that explains the multitude of puzzling phenomena in the Universe.

Another question of interest to scientists is, of course, the future of the Universe. Here there are two possible scenarios: either the Universe will continue to expand indefinitely and at some very distant time the galaxies will have drifted so far apart that the inhabitants of one won't be able to see any of the others, or at some moment the scattering of the galaxies will be arrested and they will begin to come closer to one another. Computations show that which of these tendencies will prevail depends on the average density of matter in the Universe. If this density is less than 10^{-29}g/cm^3, then expansion will continue forever. Otherwise, at some moment, the Universe will begin to contract. Some scientists believe that the contraction will continue until the Universe will again achieve the state of a superdense clot and the same chain of events will again unfold. One cannot help but remember the words of Heraclitus about the fire that regularly blazes up and is regularly extinguished.

And what, in fact, is the density of matter in the Universe? What makes it difficult to answer this question is the possibility that a great part of matter is in a state that makes observations impossible. (Here we mention black holes that emit no radiation, intergalactic gas, and possibly neutrinos that can penetrate enormous masses of matter without interacting with it.) According to current estimates, this density is one-thirtieth less than the critical value, so that it seems that we need not fear that the Universe will begin to contract. But each year brings so much new knowledge that it is premature to try to give a definitive answer to this question.

Is the Universe infinite? One of the most difficult questions of cosmology is the question in the title of this section. If the average density of matter in the Metagalaxy is more than the critical value of 10^{-29}g/cm^3, then we obtain an open model of the Metagalaxy. If this density is less than 10^{-29}g/cm^3, then we obtain a closed model. Whereas the open model accords with the assumption of a Universe of infinite size, the closed model has positive curvature, and so its size is bounded from above by some number. At the moment there are no conceivable methods of disproving the claim that our Universe is closed and that its size does not exceed 10^{25} km.

The question of the finiteness or infiniteness of the Universe is further complicated by the fact that, from the viewpoint of relativity, time and space don't exist separately but only as a single entity. Using this fact, the Russian cosmologist A.L. Zel'manovich[34] constructed absolutely baffling models. In one of these models space has an infinite volume in one coordinate system and a finite volume in another. In another model, space of infinite volume in one coordinate system is part of space of finite volume in another system. There are similar paradoxes involving time and connected with observations of gravitational collapse (the shrinking of a burned-out star to a point under the action of gravity). In one coordinate system this process fits into a finite time interval and in another coordinate system it lasts infinitely long.

We see that the usual contraposition of the finite and infinite in space and the finite and infinite in time as mutually exclusive possibilities, and, quite generally, our customary formulation of questions involving the finite and the infinite in space and time cannot be regarded as correct in all cases.

Another complicating factor is the possibility of an inhomogeneous and anisotropic (having different properties in different directions) Universe. These possibilities can favor models of the Universe very different from a sphere in three-dimensional space. (Note that even surfaces of zero curvature include not only parts of the plane but also cylinders and cones.) Thus there are infinitely many admissible models of the Universe. But while the supply of models is immeasurably richer than it was before the advent of relativistic cosmology, dealing with them is immeasurably more complex than before.

All these complexities show that it is hardly possible to give a simple answer to the question posed at the beginning of this section.

The question of the infinite divisibility of matter has also become immeasurably more complicated than before. At the beginning of the 20th century it was thought that matter consisted of indivisible atoms. Then Rutherford found that atoms consist of nuclei and electrons. Next came the discovery of protons, and, a few years later, of neutrons and positrons. At the end of the thirties, the neutron-positron model of the atomic nucleus came into being. This model was so apt that it made possible the solution of the problem of the release of atomic energy. But even before the activation of the first atomic reactor came the discovery of new elementary particles – mesons of various kinds. After that, the number of elementary particles grew almost exponentially. There were antiprotons and antineutrons, various hyperions and antihyperions, resonances, and so on. Then it turned out that neutrons can change into protons and protons into neutrons, so that for these particles the term "consists of" lost all meaning.

To bring order into the world of elementary particles, quarks, particles of a new kind, were devised. While they can be used to explain everything in a satisfactory manner, no one has observed them. Quarks differ by *color* (this term is strictly a convention). This led to a new branch of physics – *chromodynamics*. According to very recent views we will never see "live" quarks. The reason for this is that inside elementary particles the forces that bind quarks increase with the distance between them (much as stretching a spring increases its tension). All this shows that it is difficult to say how one should, at this point, think of the infinite divisibility of matter.

Chapter 2

The mysteries of infinite sets

A concept without definition. Pythagoras, Zeno, Plato, and Aristotle all discussed the one and the many. One Pythagorean defined a (natural) number as a collection of units, and in Book VII of the *Elements* Euclid writes that "Number is a collection consisting of units" (in ancient Greek mathematics one was not regarded as a number).

But the "set-theoretic boom," that is, the wide use of set theory in various areas of science and technology, came only in the 20th century. Why was it possible to get along without this concept before? There is a simple answer to this question: those who did not know about sets resembled Molière's hero who did not know that he spoke prose. They dealt with sets all the time but did not refer to them as such. For example, an economist planning the connections between departments in a factory did not think about each individual machine tool but about, say, all lathes or milling machines and about their output. Similarly, an officer of a certain rank preparing a military operation thought of the actions of his whole company, batallion, regiment or division and not of the actions of individual soldiers. All these people worked with sets of objects, studied them as single collectivities. A mathematician would say that they dealt with sets of elements and not with individual elements.

Unfortunately, he could not have said what a set is. When defining a new concept mathematicians reduce it to known concepts. But one must start somewhere, and there is no concept in mathematics more basic than a set.

This is not surprising if we bear in mind that almost all sciences begin with classification, with grouping of similar objects or concepts into a single whole and with separating of dissimilar objects. Before there can be biology, people must learn to tell a wolf from a jackal and a rabbit from a hare. Before there can be mineralogy people must for centuries collect stones and tell granite from flint and malachite from jasper. From the viewpoint of mathematics all classification reduces to forming sets on the basis of certain criteria. That's why it is impossible to reduce the concepts of a set to simpler concepts.

We can speak of the set of chairs in a room, of the set of protons on Jupiter, of the set of words in the works of Pushkin, of the set of cells in a human body, of the set of fish in an ocean, of the set of natural numbers, of the set of points in the plane, of the set of spheres in space, and so on.

The objects that make up a set are called its *elements*. The examples just mentioned show that elements can be real objects (chairs, protons, fish, and so on) as well as abstract objects (numbers, points, geometric figures, and so on). Elements can also be such figments of the human imagination as mythological heroes, ghosts and the gods of various religions.

A set of real objects is usually *finite* – that is, contains finitely many elements. Finite sets are usually given by listing their elements. For example, the set of days in the week is given by the list {Monday, Tuesday, Wednesday, Thursday, Friday, Saturday, Sunday}. Of course, it is hardly possible to list the elements of large sets such as fish in an ocean or grains of sand at the seashore.

Sets of abstract concepts or mythological heroes and gods can also be finite. Examples of such sets are the set of even primes, the set of Olympic gods, and so on. The set of natural numbers is infinite, and so is the set of points in the plane.

Braces that contain a list of elements of a set symbolize the uniting of these elements into a single whole. If an element a belongs to a set A then we write $a \in A$. If an element a does not belong to a set A then we write $a \notin A$. For example, if $\mathbf{N}$ is the set of natural numbers, then $6 \in \mathbf{N}$, $3/4 \notin \mathbf{N}$ and crocodile $\notin \mathbf{N}$. If A is the set of months in the year then May $\in A$ and Wednesday $\notin A$.

Thus when speaking of a set we unite certain elements or concepts in a single whole and then operate with this whole. The German mathematician Georg Cantor,[1] the creator of set theory, put it thus: "A set is a Many which allows itself to be thought of by us as a One."

The academician N.N. Luzin,[2] one of the founders of the Russian set-theoretic school, suggested the following intuitive representation of a set. Think of a transparent, impenetrable shell, something like a transparent and tightly closed bag. Suppose that the shell contains all the elements of some set A and no others. This shell and the objects in it can serve as a representation of the set A consisting of these elements. The transparent shell that contains all the elements of the set and no others represents the act of uniting the elements that gives rise to the set A.

Sets and properties of objects. One cannot list the elements of an infinite set. Nor is it practical to list the elements of a very large finite set. To determine a set of either kind we specify a property shared by all of its elements and not belonging to any element not in the set. Such a property of the elements of a set is called its *characteristic* property.

For example, a characteristic property of the set of prime (natural) numbers is that all its elements have exactly two divisors. Using this property we can immediately tell that neither 1, nor 18, nor 2/3 are primes. Indeed, 1 has just one divisor, 18 has six (1,2,3,6,9,18), and 2/3 is not a natural number. On the other hand, 7 is a prime because it has exactly two divisors, 1 and 7.

The philosophers of antiquity tried hard to find characteristic properties of various sets. For example, Plato is said to have given the following definition: "A human is a live featherless biped." The story has it that his contemporary Diogenes plucked a rooster and said: "Here is Plato's human." This forced Plato to add "with wide toe nails" to his definition. This too was an obviously specious characteristic property of the concept of a human.

We write $P(x)$ for "the element x has the property P," and $\{x \mid P(x)\}$ for the set of elements each of which has the property P. For example, $A = \{x \mid x^2 - 3x + 2 = 0\}$ consists of all roots of the equation $x^2 - 3x + 2 = 0$, and $B = \{x \mid x \in \mathbf{N} \text{ and } 0 < x < 3\}$ consists of all natural numbers that satisfy the inequality $0 < x < 3$. These sets both consist of the numbers 1 and 2, that is they have the same elements. We call such sets *equal* and write $A = B = \{1, 2\}$. This example shows that while the concepts of set and characteristic property are closely related, they are not the same – the same set can be given by means of different characteristic properties. Characteristic properties that describe the same set are usually called *equivalent*.

Many mathematical theorems concern the equality of two sets, say, of the set of natural numbers divisible by 3 and the set of natural numbers (written in decimal notation) such that the sum of their digits is divisible by 3, or, for another example, of the set of equilateral triangles and the set of equiangular triangles. Some problems of this kind are still open. For example, we don't know whether the set of natural numbers n for which the equation $x^n + y^n = z^n$ has solutions in $\mathbf{N}$ (= the set of natural numbers) is equal to the set $\{1, 2\}$ (*Fermat's Last Theorem*), or, for another example, whether the set of primes p for which $2^p - 1$ is divisible by p^2 is equal to the set $\{1093, 3511\}$.

Sets and the real world. Set-theoretic methods are now used in all areas of learning. For example, linguists study the set of letters or the set of (grammatical) cases of a language, ethnographers study the set of forms of family relations of members of a tribe, and physicists study the set of molecules in a given volume of a gas.

All these sets are finite. In many cases they can be given by listing their elements. For example, a teacher lists the students in his class in the class roster, a librarian catalogues the set of books in her library, and a geographer lists the set of states on the earth.

The progress of physics has demonstrated the growing difficulty of describing particles in terms of set theory. This is due to the fact that many particles transmute into one another. For example, a proton can transmute into a neutron and conversely, so that here the term "consists of" loses its intuitive sense.

When making up sets of objects of the real world it is frequently necessary to identify various objects or concepts. For example, the maker of a dictionary ignores the fact that a word is pronounced differently in different parts of a country. To her, variations of pronunciation are irrelevant. What counts is the underlying single element of the set of words of the language involved. (The student of dialects looks very differently at the same set. What interests her most is precisely the different pronunciations of a single word.)

Thus in talking about elements of a set (of real objects or of abstract notions) we employ a kind of identification operation and feel intuitively that it won't lead to contradictions. In other words, sets arise from vaguer concepts by identification of various elements.

Other complications involved in the use of set-theoretic concepts in the study of the real world are due to the vagueness of many concepts, the indefiniteness of many properties of objects, and the difficulty of splitting reality into distinct objects. Some of these difficulties are discussed below.

Of course, all the indicated complications and difficulties are no reason for not using set-theoretic methods in describing reality or in constructing scientific theories. They do show, however, that the set-theoretic treatment of an area of science imposes serious limitations on our approach to the investigated phenomena, and in many cases "crudifies" them.

On the positive side, as noted by Yu. I. Manin,[3] the concepts of set theory are very useful for constructing mathematical models of phenomena in the real world, because they have laid a universal foundation for defining all mathematical constructions using ... "generalized geometric images." These mental constructs represent both a receptacle for the meaning of mathematical formalisms and a means of extracting meaningful assertions from the vast sea of derivable mathematical formulas.

They are therefore natural intermediaries between mathematics and physics. In Manin's view, another advantage of set-theoretic language is that it forces one to avoid all that is superfluous.

Sets and language. We noted earlier that prescribing sets of real objects by means of their characteristic properties involves various difficulties. These difficulties stem from the large number of intermediate forms and from the imprecision of everyday language.

For example, consider the term *the set of planets in the Solar system*. We claim that this term is not fully defined. For one thing, we do not know whether or not there are planets beyond Pluto. For another, in addition to the major planets – Mercury, Venus, the Earth, Mars, Jupiter, Saturn, Uranus, Neptune, and Pluto – some 1600 small planets, the so-called asteroids, revolve around the Sun. The diameters of some of them, Ceres, Pallas and Juno, say, measure hundreds of kilometers. On the other hand, there are asteroids whose diameters do not exceed 1 km. With improved methods of observation astronomers are certain to discover celestial objects of ever smaller dimensions, and the question will be asked where planets end and meteorites and cosmic dust begin.[*]

Fuzzy sets. The American scientist L. Zadeh[4] found an original way out of the difficulties just described. Zadeh introduced the concept of a *fuzzy set* and the closely related concept of a *linguistic variable*. Just as with precise properties (being a prime, being a triangle) there are associated ordinary or *precise sets*, so too with fuzzy properties (being a young person, being a long street) there are associated fuzzy sets (of young persons, of long streets). For example, a distinguished academician will likely refer to a forty-year-old colleague as a

---

[*]At this point, in the last paragraph of this section, the author notes that the difference between planets and meteorites is of interest only to astronomers and is not of great importance. On the other hand, he says, there are compelling reasons for precision in, say, the classification of crimes. I agree, but left out this paragraph because it strikes me as irrelevant.

I also left out the first two paragraphs of this section because they deal with the term *the set of Russian words* and its imprecision. It is clear that it makes little sense to translate this material. On the other hand, I am sure that English readers will have no difficulty in spotting some elements of imprecision in the term *the set of English words*. (Translator)

young person whereas a first-year student will likely regard his forty-year-old professor as elderly. With every person (or, more precisely, with every "expert") there is associated a precise set of people he or she regards as young. But then with every person x there is associated a number m/n, where n is the number of all experts and m is the number of experts who regard x as young. We denote m/n by $p(x)$ and say that x belongs to the fuzzy set of young people with *membership coefficient* $p(x)$. Of course, the latter takes on values from 0 to 1.

Precise sets differ from fuzzy sets in that for them $p(x)$ can take on just two values, namely 0 if $x \notin A$ and 1 if $x \in A$. The existence of experts makes it possible to form a fuzzy set from the set of precise sets associated with each expert. Of course, notwithstanding the fuzziness of the set of young people, we can say with certainty that for some x, $p(x) = 1$ (for example, no one will deny that a newborn is young) and for certain other x, $p(x) = 0$ (for example, no one will call an 80-year-old young). No one? Well, there is the story that when the 65-year-old chessmaster Tartakover defeated the 70-year-old chessmaster Bernstein he exclaimed "youth wins!"

Of course, it makes little sense to call a commission of experts every time to determine "membership coefficients." For the most part such coefficients are introduced differently, on the basis, say, of statistical data. But once they have been selected, they can be used to obtain membership coefficients for other sets.

The notion of a fuzzy set led to the introduction of fuzzy relations and fuzzy algorithms. But fuzzy algorithms had been in use long before they were defined by Zadeh. Every cookbook contains algorithms with advice such as this: "First whip the cream until it is very thick. Then add the flour and whip the mixture well. . ." True, authors of cookbooks don't define precisely when the whipped cream is very thick and how much whipping is appropriate. But there are good reasons for thinking that dishes prepared according to such recipes usually turn out all right. It is interesting that fuzzy algorithms are now beginning to be used in, for example, mathematical computing. Still, only the future will determine the suitability and usefulness of Zadeh's way of introducing fuzzy sets.

Infinite sets. What we said earlier about sets referred for the most part to finite sets. For millennia the study of infinite sets was kept out of science on Aristotle's authority. But in the 13th century the Schoolman Robert Grosseteste, a professor at Oxford (and the teacher of the famous Roger Bacon) declared that the actually infinite is a definite number, and while it is beyond our cognition it actually exists. Grosseteste thought that infinities can be compared with one another; that there are more moments in a larger time interval than in a smaller one; that there are more points in a larger magnitude than in a smaller one; and that the number "of points in a segment one ell long" is its true measure. Thus Aristotle's potential infinite was again opposed by the actual infinite of units.

The gradual use of the actual infinite began in the 18th century (infinite series were actually viewed as sums of infinitely many terms), and in the 19th century Gauss, supposedly so very much against the use of the actual infinite in mathematics, used it in his number-theoretic work. More explicit uses of the actual infinite are found in the works of some of Gauss' successors such as Dirichlet[5] and Dedekind.[6]

However, there was almost no systematic study of infinite sets. *Paradoxes of the infinite*, by the Czech philosopher and mathematician Bernard Bolzano,[7] appeared posthumously in 1851. In this book, Bolzano made the first attempt to study the properties of the actually infinite. The book anticipated many concepts of the theory of infinite sets, but these anticipations lacked the precision and clarity that Georg Cantor endowed them with in his works written over a period of twenty years.

In connection with his study of infinite series of trigonometric functions Cantor faced the need to classify in a certain sense sets made up of points of a straight line (now briefly referred to as *point sets*). In particular, he wished to know if all such sets can be listed. In the course of these investigations he realized that finite and infinite sets have radically different properties. In particular, he noticed that operations that are impossible in the case of finite sets can be easily realized for infinite sets. For example, try to put up additional guests in a hotel all of whose rooms already have a single guest, without any doubling up or evictions. Impossible? Only if the hotel is finite! And what if it has infinitely many rooms?... Such hotels are found in the stories of the intergalactic wanderer Ion the Quiet, and it is only right that we should give him the floor.

The extraordinary hotel, or the thousand and first journey of Ion the Quiet. I got home rather late – the get-together at the club Andromeda Nebula dragged on long after midnight. I was tormented by nightmares the whole night. I dreamt that I had swallowed an enormous Kurdl; then I dreamt that I was again on the planet Durditov and didn't know how to escape one of those terrible machines they have there that turn people into hexagons; then ... People generally advise against mixing old age with seasoned mead. An unexpected telephone call brought me back to reality. It was my old friend and companion in interstellar travels Professor Tarantog.

"A pressing problem, my dear Ion," I heard. "Astronomers have discovered a strange object in the cosmos – a mysterious black line stretching from one galaxy to another. No one knows what is going on. Even the best telescopes and radio-telescopes placed on rockets cannot help in unraveling the mystery. You are our last hope. Fly right away in the direction of nebula ACD-1587."

The next day I got my old photon rocket back from the repair shop and installed in it my time accelerator and my electronic robot who knows all the languages of the cosmos and all the stories about interstellar travel (it is guaranteed to keep me entertained for at least a five-year journey). Then I took off to attend to the matter at hand.

Just as the robot exhausted his entire supply of stories and had begun to repeat himself (nothing is worse than listening to an electronic robot repeating an old story for the tenth time), the goal of my journey appeared in the distance. The galaxies which covered up the mysterious line lay behind me, and in front of me was ... the hotel Cosmos. Some time ago I constructed a small planet for wandering interstellar exiles, but they tore it apart and again were without a refuge. After that, they decided to give up wandering into foreign galaxies and to put up a grandiose building – a hotel for all travelers in the cosmos. This hotel extended across almost all the galaxies. I say "almost all" because the exiles dismantled a few uninhabited galaxies and made off with a few poorly situated constellations from each of the remaining ones.

But they did a marvelous job of building the hotel. In each room there were faucets from which hot and cold plasma flowed. If you wished, you could be split into atoms for the night, and in the morning the porter would put your atoms back together again.

But, most important of all, there was an *infinite number of rooms* in the hotel. The exiles hoped that from now on no one would have to hear that irksome phrase that had plagued them during their time of wandering: "no room available."

In spite of this I had no luck. The first thing that caught my eye when I entered the vestibule of the hotel was a sign: Delegates to the cosmic zoologists' congress are to register on the 127th floor.

Since cosmic zoologists came from all the galaxies and there are an infinite number of these, it turned out that all the rooms were occupied by participants in the conference. There was no place for me. True, the manager tried to get some of the delegates to agree to double up so that I could share a room with one of them. But when I found out that one proposed roommate breathed fluorine and another considered it normal to have the temperature of his environment at about 860°, I politely turned down such "pleasant" neighbors.

Luckily the director of the hotel had been an exile and well remembered the good turn I had done him and his fellows. He would try to find me a place at the hotel. After all, you could catch pneumonia spending the night in interstellar space. After some meditation, he turned to the manager and said:

"Put him in number 1."

"Where am I going to put the guest in number 1?"

"Put him in number 2. Shift the guest in number 2 to number 3, number 3 to number 4, and so on."

It was only at this point that I began to appreciate the unusual qualities of the hotel. If there had been only a finite number of rooms, the guest in the last room would have had to move out into interstellar space. But because the hotel had infinitely many rooms, there was space for all, and I was able to move in without depriving any of the cosmic zoologists of his room.

The following morning, I was not astonished to find that I was asked to move into number 1,000,000. It was simply that some cosmic zoologists had arrived belatedly from galaxy VSK-3472, and they had to find room for another 999,999 guests. But while I was going to the manager to pay for my room on the third day of my stay at the hotel, I was dismayed to see that from the manager's window there extended a line whose end disappeared somewhere near the clouds of Magellan. Just then I heard a voice:

"I will exchange two stamps from the Andromeda nebula for a stamp from Sirius."

"Who has the Whale stamp from the 57th year of the cosmic era?"

I turned in bewilderment to the manager and asked:

"Who are these people?"

"This is the interstellar congress of philatelists."

"Are there many of them?"

"An infinite set – one representative from each galaxy."

"But how will you find room for them? After all, the cosmic zoologists don't leave till tomorrow."

"I don't know; I am on my way now to speak to the director about it for a few minutes."

However, this time the problem turned out to be much more difficult and the few minutes extended into an hour. Finally, the manager left the office of the director and proceeded to make his arrangements. First he asked the guest in number 1 to move to number 2. This seemed strange to me, since I knew from my own experience that such a shift would only free one room, whereas he had to find places for nothing less than an infinite set of philatelists. But the manager continued to give orders:

"Put the guest from number 2 into number 4, the one from number 3 into number 6; in general, put the guest from number n into number $2n$."

Now his plan became clear: by this scheme he would free the infinite set of odd-numbered rooms and would be able to settle the philatelists in them. So in the end the even numbers turned out to be occupied by cosmic zoologists and the odd numbers by philatelists. (I didn't say anything about myself – after three days of acquaintance I became so friendly with the cosmic zoologists that I had been chosen an honorary representative to their congress; so I had to abandon my own room along with all the cosmic zoologists and move from number 1,000,000 to number 2,000,000). And a philatelist friend of mine who was 574th in line got room number 1147. In general, the philatelist who was nth in line got room number $2n - 1$.

The following day the room situation eased up – the cosmic zoologists' congress ended and they took off for home. I moved in with the director, in whose apartment there was a vacant room. But what is good for the guests does not always please the management. After a few days my generous host became sad.

"What's the trouble?" I asked him.
"Half the rooms are empty. We won't fulfill the financial plan."

Actually, I was not quite sure what financial plan he was talking about; after all, he was getting the fee for an infinite number of rooms, but I nevertheless gave him some advice:

"Well, why don't you move the guests closer together; move them around so as to fill all the rooms."

This turned out to be easy to do. The philatelists occupied only the odd rooms: 1,3,5,7,9, etc. They left the guest in number 1 alone. They moved number 3 into number 2, number 5 into number 3, number 7 into number 4, etc. At the end all the rooms were once again filled and not even one new guest had arrived.

But this did not end the director's unhappiness. It was explained that the exiles did not content themselves with the erection of the hotel Cosmos. The indefatigable builders then went on to construct an infinite set of hotels, each of which had infinitely many rooms. To do this they dismantled so many galaxies that the intergalactic equilibrium was upset and this could entail serious consequences. They were therefore asked to close all the hotels except ours and put the material used back into place. But it was difficult to carry out this order when all the hotels (ours included) were filled. He was asked to move all the guests from infinitely many hotels, each of which had infinitely many guests, into one hotel, and this one was already filled!

"I've had enough!" the director shouted. "First I put up one guest in an already full hotel, then another 999,999, then even an infinite set of guests; and now they want me to find room in it for an additional infinite set of infinite sets of guests. No, the hotel isn't made of rubber; let them put them where they want."

But an order was an order, and they had five days to get ready for the arrival of the new guests. Nobody worked in the hotel during these five days – everybody was pondering how to solve the problem. A contest was announced – the prize would be a tour of one of the galaxies. But all the solutions proposed were turned down as unsuccessful. Then a cook in training made the following proposal: leave the guest in number 1 in his present quarters, move number 2 into number 1001, number 3 into number 2001, etc. After this, put the guest from the second hotel into numbers 2, 1002, 2002, etc. of our hotel, the guests from the third hotel into numbers 3, 1003, 2003, etc. The project was turned down, for it was not clear where the guests of the 1001st hotel were to be placed; after all, the guests from the first 1000 hotels would occupy all the rooms. We recalled on this occasion that when the servile Roman senate offered to rename the month of September "Tiberius" to honor the emperor (the preceding months had already been given the names of Julius and Augustus), Tiberius asked them caustically "and what will you offer the thirteenth Caesar?"

The hotel's bookkeeper proposed a pretty good variant. He advised us to make use of the properties of the geometric progression and resettle the guests as follows: the guests from the first hotel are to be put in rooms 2, 4, 8, 16, 32, etc. (these numbers form a geometric progression with multiplier 2). The guests from the second hotel are to be put in rooms 3, 9, 27, 81, etc. (these are the terms of the geometric progression with multiplier 3). He proposed that we resettle the guests from the other hotels in a similar manner. But the director asked him:

"And we are to use the progression with multiplier 4 for the third hotel?"

"Of course," the bookkeeper replied.

"Then nothing is accomplished; after all, we already have someone from the first hotel in room 4, so where are we going to put the people from the third hotel?"

My turn to speak came; it was not for nothing that they made you study mathematics for five years at the Stellar Academy.

"Use prime numbers. Put the guests from the first hotel into numbers 2, 4, 8, 16, . . ., from the second hotel into numbers 3, 9, 27, 81, . . ., from the third into numbers 5, 25, 125, 625, . . ., the fourth into numbers 7, 49, 343, . . ."

"And it won't happen again that some room will have two guests?" the director asked.

"No. After all, if you take two prime numbers, none of their positive integer powers can equal one another. If p and q are prime numbers, $p \neq q$, and m and n are natural numbers, then $p^m \neq q^n$."

The director agreed with me and immediately found an improvement on the method I had proposed, in which only the primes 2 and 3 were needed. Namely, he proposed to put the guest from the mth room of the nth hotel into room number $2^m 3^n$. This works because if $m \neq p$ or $n \neq q$, $2^m 3^n \neq 2^p 3^q$. So no room would have two occupants.

This proposal delighted everyone. It was a solution of the problem that everyone had supposed insoluble. But neither the director nor I got the prize; too many rooms would be left unoccupied if our solutions were adopted (according to mine – such rooms as 6, 10, 12, and, more generally, all rooms whose numbers were not powers of primes, and according to the director's – all rooms whose numbers could not be written in the form $2^n 3^m$). The best solution was proposed by one of the philatelists, the president of the Academy of Mathematics of the galaxy Swan.

He proposed that we construct a tabulation, in whose rows the number of the hotel would appear, and in whose columns the room numbers would appear. For example, at the intersection of the 4th row and the 6th column there would appear the 6th room of the 4th hotel. Here is the tabulation (actually, only its upper left part, for to write down the entire tabulation we would have to employ infinitely many rows and columns):

$$(1,1) \quad (1,2) \quad (1,3) \quad (1,4) \quad (1,5) \quad \ldots \quad (1,n) \quad \ldots$$

$$(2,1) \quad (2,2) \quad (2,3) \quad (2,4) \quad (2,5) \quad \ldots \quad (2,n) \quad \ldots$$

$$(3,1) \quad (3,2) \quad (3,3) \quad (3,4) \quad (3,5) \quad \ldots \quad (3,n) \quad \ldots$$

$$(4,1) \quad (4,2) \quad (4,3) \quad (4,4) \quad (4,5) \quad \ldots \quad (4,n) \quad \ldots$$

$$(5,1) \quad (5,2) \quad (5,3) \quad (5,4) \quad (5,5) \quad \ldots \quad (5,n) \quad \ldots$$

$$\ldots \ldots \ldots \ldots \ldots \ldots \ldots \ldots \ldots \ldots \ldots \ldots \ldots \ldots \ldots \ldots$$

$$(m,1) \quad (m,2) \quad (m,3) \quad (m,4) \quad (m,5) \quad \ldots \quad (m,n) \quad \ldots$$

$$\ldots \ldots \ldots \ldots \ldots \ldots \ldots \ldots \ldots \ldots \ldots \ldots \ldots \ldots \ldots \ldots$$

"And now settle the guests according to squares," the mathematician-philatelist said.

"How?" The director did not understand.

"By squares. In number 1 put the guest from $(1,1)$, i.e., from the first room of the first hotel; in number 2 put the guest from $(1,2)$, i.e., from the second room of the first hotel; in number 3 put the guest from $(2,2)$, the second room of the second hotel, and in number 4 – the guest from $(2,1)$, the first room of the second hotel. We will thus have settled the guests from the upper left square of side 2. After this, put the guest from $(1,3)$ in number 5, from $(2,3)$ in number 6, from $(3,3)$ in number 7, from $(3,2)$ in number 8, from $(3,1)$ in number 9. (These rooms fill out the square of side 3.) And we carry on in this way:

(1,1)		(1,2)		(1,3)		(1,4)		(1,5)	...	(1,n)	...
		↓		↓		↓		↓		↓	
(2,1)	←	(2,2)		(2,3)		(2,4)		(2,5)	...	(2,n)	...
				↓		↓		↓		↓	
(3,1)	←	(3,2)	←	(3,3)		(3,4)		(3,5)	...	(3,n)	...
						↓		↓		↓	
(4,1)	←	(4,2)	←	(4,3)	←	(4,4)		(4,5)	...	(4,n)	...
								↓		↓	
(5,1)	←	(5,2)	←	(5,3)	←	(5,4)	←	(5,5)	...	(5,n)	...
										↓	

. . . .

(n,1)	←	(n,2)	←	(n,3)	←	(n,4)	←	(n,5)←	...	(n,n)	...

. . . .

"Will there really be enough room for all?" The director was doubtful.

"Of course. After all, according to this scheme we settle the guests from the first n rooms of the first n hotels in the first n^2 rooms. So sooner or later every guest will get a room. For example, if we are talking about the guest from number 136 in hotel number 217, he will get a room at the 217th stage. We can even easily figure out which room. It will have the number $217^2 - 136 + 1$. More generally, if the guest occupies room n in the mth hotel, then if $n \geq m$ he will occupy number $(n - 1)^2 + m$, and if $n < m$, number $m^2 - n + 1$."

The proposed project was recognized to be the best – all the guests from all hotels would find a place in our hotel, and not even one room would be empty. The mathematician-philatelist received the prize – a tour of galaxy LCR-287.

In honor of this so successful solution, the director organized a reception to which he invited all the guests. The reception, too, had its problems. The occupants of the even-numbered rooms arrived a half hour late, and when they appeared, it turned out that all the chairs were occupied, even though our kind host had arranged to have a chair for each guest. They had to wait while everyone shifted to new places so as to free the necessary quantity of seats (of course, not one new chair was brought into the hall). Later on, when they began to serve the guests ice cream, it was discovered that each guest had two portions, although, as a matter of fact, the cook had only prepared one portion per guest. I hope that by now the reader can figure out by himself how this happened.

At the end of the reception I got into my photon rocket and took off for Earth. I had to inform the cosmonauts of Earth about the new haven existing in the cosmos. Besides, I wanted to consult some prominent mathematicians and my friend Professor Tarantog about the properties of infinite sets.

From the author. With this we temporarily take leave of our hero. Many of his stories give rise to doubt – after all, according to the laws of the theory of relativity it is impossible to transmit signals at speeds greater than 186,000 miles/sec. Thus, even the very first order of the director would require an infinitely large interval of time to carry out. But let us not ask too much of Ion the Quiet – he has had even more improbable adventures during his travels.

The rest of the book is devoted to the story of the theory of sets. And although the events will no longer take place in interstellar space but on the interval [0,1] or the square of side 1, many of them will seem no less unusual.

How to compare sets in terms of size. At the beginning of this chapter we were concerned with properties of sets which hold generally for both finite and infinite sets. Here we shall be interested in properties characteristic of infinite sets alone. We have already seen in the story of Ion the Quiet that these properties are quite different from those of finite sets – things impossible for finite sets turn out to be possible for infinite sets.

The first question which we shall now discuss is the problem of deciding when two infinite sets are of equal size. For finite sets of the most varied types we can always say which of them contains the larger number of elements. This problem is much more complicated for infinite sets. For example, which is the larger set, that of the natural numbers or that of the rational numbers? That of the rational numbers or that of the real numbers? Are there more points on the entire line than there are on a segment? More points in a square than on a line?

It appears quite simple at first glance to answer these questions. After all, the set of natural numbers is only a part of the set of rational numbers and the segment is only a part of the line. Isn't it obvious, therefore, that there are fewer natural numbers than there are rational numbers and that there are fewer points on a segment than on the line? It turns out not to be so obvious. It does not follow at all that when we go from finite to infinite sets, the laws derived from the study of the former, for example, a law such as "the part is less than the whole," remain valid.

Above all, an attempt to compare infinite sets using the criterion that one is a part of the other is doomed to failure in advance. For example, where are there more points, in a square or on the whole of an infinite line? After all, the square cannot be contained in a line and, without breaking it, it is impossible to put a line inside a square. Of course, it is possible to break the line up into segments of length equal to the side of the square, and after that place each segment inside the square in such a way that no two intersect. But how do we know that we can find a way to break up the square so that the parts can be strung out along the line without overlapping? And how many infinite sets there are which are not parts of one another! The set of squares in the plane and the set of circles in the same plane do not have even a single element in common. How can we compare them? How can we find out if there are more atoms of nitrogen or of oxygen in the universe?

We have now posed the problem. First we investigate under what conditions it can be said that one set contains just as many elements as another. In other words, we study the conditions under which two infinite sets have "the same measure" of elements.

On the dance floor. The problem of comparison is easily solved for finite sets. In order to find out if the number of elements is the same for two sets, we have only to count them. If we get the same numbers, this means that both sets have the same size. But such a procedure is not suitable for infinite sets; for, having begun to count the elements of an infinite set, we run the risk of devoting our entire lives to this job and still not completing the enterprise we have undertaken.

And the method of counting is not always convenient even for finite sets. For instance, let us go to a dance hall. How can we tell if the numbers of boys and girls here are the same? Of course, we could ask the boys to go off to one side and the girls to the other, and undertake to count both groups. But, in the first place, this would give us superfluous information; we are not interested in how many boys and girls are here, but only in whether the numbers are the same. And then, the young people on the dance floor did not get together to stand around and wait for the end of the count, but to dance.

Well, what then? Let us satisfy their wish and ask the orchestra to play a dance that everybody knows how to do. Then the boys will ask the girls to dance and. . . our problem will be solved. After all, if it turns out that all the boys and girls are dancing, i.e., if all the young people are paired off, then it is obvious that there are just as many boys as girls on the dance floor.

We could find out by an identical procedure whether the number of specta-tors in a theater is equal to the number of seats. If during the performance all the places are taken, no spectator is standing in the aisles and one spectator is sitting in each seat, then we can be sure that there are just as many spectators as seats.

For every flow there is an ebb. We have seen how it is possible to determine that two finite sets have equally many elements without having recourse to counting. We can also apply this method to infinite sets. But there we can no longer get an orchestra to do the job; we ourselves have to distribute the elements of the two sets to be compared into "couples."

Suppose we are given two sets A and B. We shall say that we have established a *one-to-one correspondence* between them, if the elements of these sets have been joined in pairs (a, b) such that:

(1) element a belongs to set A, and element b belongs to set B;

(2) every element of the two sets occurs in one and only one pair.

For instance, if set A consists of the boys on the dance floor and set B consists of the girls found there, then pair (a, b) is composed of the boy and girl dancing together. If set A consists of the spectators and set B consists of the seats in the theater, then pair (a, b) is composed of the spectator and the seat in which he sits. The reader can easily think of other examples of correspondences between sets of the same size.

Naturally, not every correspondence between sets is one-to-one. If set A consists of all the trees in the world and set B consists of all the fruit growing on these trees, then we can set up the following correspondence between these sets: to each fruit we make correspond the tree on which it grows. But this is not a one-to-one correspondence: on some trees many pieces of fruit grow, while other trees do not even bear fruit. Thus, some elements a (trees) will appear in many pairs, while other elements a will not appear in any.

For two finite sets, it means the same thing to say that there is a one-to-one correspondence between them, or to say that they have equally many elements. The fundamental turning point in the theory of sets came when Cantor decided to compare infinite sets in the same manner.

In other words, Cantor said that two (possibly infinite) sets A and B have equally many elements, if it is possible to set up a one-to-one correspondence between them.

Mathematicians do not usually say: "sets A and B have equally many elements"; they say: "A and B have the same *cardinality*" or they say: "sets A and B are *equivalent*."

Because of this, the word *cardinality* means the same thing for infinite sets as the words "number of elements" do for finite sets.

The Czech savant B. Bolzano arrived at the notion of one-to-one correspondence independently of Cantor; but he gave up further pursuit of the idea because of the difficulties into which it led him. As we shall soon see, we shall have to set aside many cherished habits of thought once we accept the principle of comparing infinite sets with the aid of the one-to-one correspondence.

Can a part be equal to the whole? One dogma that we have to brush aside is the statement, established at the beginning of the development of mathematics: *a part is less than the whole.* This statement is indisputably true for finite sets, but it loses its force when we try to apply it to infinite sets. Let us recall how the director of the extraordinary hotel shifted the cosmic zoologists to even-numbered rooms. He moved the inhabitant of room n to room $2n$. In other words, he moved them according to the following scheme:

$$
\begin{array}{ccccccc}
1 & 2 & 3 & \ldots & n & \ldots \\
\downarrow & \downarrow & \downarrow & & \downarrow & \\
2 & 4 & 6 & \ldots & 2n & \ldots
\end{array}
$$

But this scheme sets up a one-to-one correspondence between the set of natural numbers

$$1, 2, 3, \ldots, n, \ldots$$

and a part of this set: the set of even numbers

$$2, 4, 6, \ldots, 2n, \ldots$$

But we agreed to assume that two sets contain equally many elements if it is possible to set up a one-to-one correspondence between them. This means that the set of natural numbers contains as many and only as many elements as one of its subsets, the set of even numbers.

In exactly the same way we could set up a one-to-one correspondence between the set of natural numbers and the set of numbers of the form

$$10, 100, 1000, 10000, \ldots$$

To do this we need only associate the natural number n with the number 10^n:

$$n \to 10^n.$$

This establishes the desired one-to-one correspondence. In the same way we can set up a one-to-one correspondence between the set of all natural numbers and the set of all squares of natural numbers:

$$n \rightarrow n^2,$$

the set of all cubes of natural numbers:

$$n \rightarrow n^3,$$

and so on.

Generally speaking, we can set up a one-to-one correspondence between the set of all natural numbers and any of its infinite subsets. To do this we need only write down the numbers of this subset in a sequence.

Incidentally, there are good reasons why they say that there is nothing new under the sun and the new is the quite forgotten old. Already at the beginning of the 17th century Galileo pondered the paradoxes of the infinite and noticed that one can set up a one-to-one correspondence between the natural numbers and their squares. His book *Discourses and mathematical proofs, concerning two new sciences pertaining to mechanics and local motions* (1638) contains a dialogue in which Salviati, expressing the ideas of Galileo, says the following:

> What we said pertains to a number of difficulties that arise because, when we use our limited powers of reasoning to discuss the infinite, we ascribe to it properties we know from things finite and bounded. But this is wrong, for properties such as a greater and a lesser magnitude and equality are not applicable to the infinite, of which we cannot say that one infinity is greater or smaller than another, or that it is equal to it.

To prove his idea, Salviati notes that, on the one hand,

> there are as many squares as there are roots, for every square has its root and every root its square; no square can have more than one root and no root more than one square... [*]   Also, there are as many roots as there are numbers, for there is no number that cannot be a root of some square; this being so, we must admit that there are as many squares as there are numbers...

---

[*] We are talking of just the natural numbers.

But on the other hand,

> the quantity of all numbers – squares and nonsquares – is greater
> than that of squares alone,

also,

> as we go to large numbers, the number of squares decreases con-
> tinually and very quickly.

According to Salviati, there is just one way of avoiding this contradiction:

> I see no other solution than to admit that there are infinitely many
> numbers, infinitely many squares, and infinitely many roots. One
> cannot say that there are fewer squares than numbers or more num-
> bers than squares: in the final analysis, the properties of equality,
> and of being a larger or a smaller magnitude, are applicable only
> to finite quantities and not when dealing with the infinite.

This shows that, in essence, Galileo was aware of the notion of a one-to-
one correspondence and realized that such a correspondence can be established
between all the natural numbers and the squares, and that these sets can therefore
be said to have the same number of elements. He also realized that in the case of
an infinite set a part can be equal to the whole. But then he jumped to the false
conclusion that all infinities are the same. This is true of the infinite subsets of
the set of natural numbers, the elements of each of which can be enumerated.

Galileo could not imagine that the set of points of an interval cannot be
enumerated (we will prove this below). Like the ancient atomists, he assumed
that an interval consists of infinitely many atoms that can be enumerated.

Countable sets. We call sets with as many elements as the set of natural
numbers *countable sets*. In other words, a set is called countable if it is infinite
and its elements can be counted with the aid of the natural numbers. For
example, the set of even numbers, the set of odd numbers, the set of primes,
and, in general, any infinite subset of the natural numbers are countable sets.

We sometimes have to employ considerable ingenuity in order to show that
this or that set is countable. Let us take as our example the set of all integers
(both positive and negative):

$$\ldots, -n, \ldots, -3, -2, -1, 0, 1, 2, 3, \ldots, n, \ldots$$

If we try to number them beginning at some given place, we find that the numbering is incomplete; for all the numbers occurring before the given place have not been counted. In order not to leave out any numbers we have to write the set in two lines:

$$0, \quad 1, \quad 2, \quad 3, \quad 4, \quad 5, \quad 6,\ldots$$
$$-1, \quad -2, \quad -3, \quad -4, \quad -5, \quad -6, \quad -7,\ldots$$

and number by columns. Here 0 is assigned the number 1, -1 is assigned the number 2, 1 the number 3, -2 the number 4, etc. In other words, zero and all the positive integers are numbered with odd numbers, while all the negative integers are numbered with even numbers. This resembles the way the hotel director placed the philatelists in a hotel already filled with cosmic zoologists.

But if it is easy to show that the set of integers is countable, it is more difficult to show that the same is true of the rational numbers. After all, the rationals are densely distributed: between any two rational numbers we can still find infinitely many rational numbers. So it is quite unclear how we should go about numbering them; it would seem that between any two numbers we would still have to number an infinite set, so that the process would never end. And it really is impossible to write down the rationals in a sequence in which each number is greater than its predecessor.

But if we do not concern ourselves about the magnitude of the numbers in our sequence, we can succeed in numbering them. Let us first write down all positive fractions with denominator 1, then all positive fractions with denominator 2, then with denominator 3, and so on. We get a tabulation like the following:

$$\frac{1}{1}, \quad \frac{2}{1}, \quad \frac{3}{1}, \quad \frac{4}{1}, \quad \frac{5}{1}, \ldots$$

$$\frac{1}{2}, \quad \frac{2}{2}, \quad \frac{3}{2}, \quad \frac{4}{2}, \quad \frac{5}{2}, \ldots$$

$$\frac{1}{3}, \quad \frac{2}{3}, \quad \frac{3}{3}, \quad \frac{4}{3}, \quad \frac{5}{3}, \ldots$$

$$\frac{1}{4}, \quad \frac{2}{4}, \quad \frac{3}{4}, \quad \frac{4}{4}, \quad \frac{5}{4}, \ldots$$

$$\frac{1}{5}, \quad \frac{2}{5}, \quad \frac{3}{5}, \quad \frac{4}{5}, \quad \frac{5}{5}, \ldots$$

$$\ldots \quad \ldots \quad \ldots \quad \ldots \quad \quad \ldots$$

Clearly, every positive rational number will appear in this table, and more than once. For example, the number 3 occurs in the form of the fractions 3/1, 6/2, 9/3, and so on.

Now we commence the numbering. For this we recall the last exploit of the director of the extraordinary hotel, the one in which he found places for the guests of infinitely many such hotels. In doing this he numbered by squares. We shall proceed in the same manner, but with this complication: we shall leave out some of the fractions (for example, since 1/1 is assigned number 1, we drop the fractions 2/2, 3/3, etc. for they express the same number). We get the following enumeration of the positive rationals: 1, 2, 1/2, 3, 3/2, 2/3, 1/3, 4, 4/3, 3/4, 1/4,....

Thus we can number all the positive rationals. It is now easy to explain how *all* the rational numbers (both positive and negative) can be numbered. We separate them into two tables, using even numbers to number one table and odd numbers for the other (remembering to reserve a number for zero).

In general, if we take the union of a countable set of countable sets, we again get a countable set. We could prove this by using this same technique of numbering by squares.

Algebraic numbers. We managed to enumerate all rational numbers. The rational numbers are obtained from the integers by using the operation of division. Now we consider the set of numbers obtained from the integers by using the algebraic operations and the extraction of roots. This set includes numbers such as $\sqrt[3]{2}+1$, $\sqrt[4]{3-\sqrt{5}}$ and "monsters" such as

$$\sqrt[7]{\frac{\sqrt[15]{147+\sqrt{3}}-\sqrt[14]{6+\sqrt{2}}}{\sqrt[21]{289}-\sqrt[5]{4+\sqrt{2}}+1}}.$$

We ask: Can one enumerate the numbers in this set? This seems more difficult than enumerating the rationals. But it turns out that this set of numbers is countable, that is, its elements can be enumerated.

To prove this we note that every number of our set is a root of an equation of the form

$$a_0x^n + a_1x^{n-1} + \cdots + a_n = 0, \tag{1}$$

where $a_0, \ldots, a_n$ are integers. For example, 3/7 is a root of $7x - 3 = 0$, $\sqrt[3]{5}$ is a root of $x^3 - 5 = 0$, and $\sqrt{2 + \sqrt[3]{3}}$ is a root of $x^6 - 6x^4 + 12x^2 - 11 = 0$. It is sometimes difficult, but always possible, to write down an equation of which a particular one of the numbers we consider is a root.

We note that not all roots of equations of the form (1) with $a_0, \ldots, a_n$ integers can be obtained from the integers by means of the algebraic operations and extraction of roots. For example, the roots of

$$x^5 - 3x + 3 = 0$$

are not so obtainable, or, as we say, this equation is not solvable in radicals. The numbers that are roots of equations of the form (1) with integer coefficients are called *algebraic numbers*. Thus the set of algebraic numbers contains the set of numbers obtained from the integers by means of algebraic operations and extraction of roots. If the former set can be shown to be countable, then so can the latter.

Note that if we manage to enumerate all algebraic equations of the form (1), then our job is almost done. Recall that every algebraic equation of degree n has at most n roots. If we manage to enumerate all equations with integer coefficients, then we can set up a table whose first row consists of the distinct roots of the first equation, the second row of the distinct roots of the second equation not in the first row, the third row of the distinct roots of the third equation not in the first two rows, and so on. The result is a table of the form

$$a_1, a_2, \ldots, a_k$$
$$b_1, b_2, \ldots, b_\ell$$
$$\cdots\cdots\cdots\cdots$$
$$c_1, c_2, \ldots, c_m$$
$$\cdots\cdots\cdots\cdots$$

It is obvious how to enumerate the elements of this table.

Now we set about enumerating the elements of the set of algebraic equations with integer coefficients. Here we imitate the scheme used by the director of the hotel in solving his most difficult problem. The one difference is that whereas the director used numbers of the form $2^m 3^n$, that is powers of two primes, we will use powers of all primes. The reader should bear in mind that every natural number is uniquely representable as the product of primes, or, equivalently, as the product of distinct prime powers.

We proceed as follows. First we enumerate the integers (see p.53). Let **a** be the number of the integer a. Then with the equation $a_0 x^n + a_1 x^{n-1} + \cdots + a_n = 0$ (where, we recall, $a_0, \ldots, a_n$ are integers) we associate the number

$$2^{a_n} 3^{a_{n-1}} \cdots p_{n+1}^{a_0}$$

(p_{n+1} is the $(n + 1)$th prime). For example, with the equation $3x^2 - 2 = 0$ we associate the number $2^4 3^1 5^7 = 3750000$; this is so because when enumerating the integers we assigned to $-2,0,3$ the numbers $4,1,7$ respectively. Now each equation has a number and different equations have different numbers. (Every number N is a unique product of prime powers. The unique exponents $a_n, a_{n-1}, \ldots, a_0$ of these prime powers determine uniquely the integers $a_n, a_{n-1}, \ldots, a_0$, and thus the equation $a_0 x^n + \cdots + a_n = 0$.)

Sets of unequal size. We have already explained what we mean when we say: "two sets have equally many elements." Now we are going to explain what we mean when we say: "one set has more elements than another." For finite sets this too can be found out without resorting to counting. Recall our example involving the dance floor. If, after the orchestra starts playing and the boys have invited the girls to dance, there are some boys leaning against the wall, then it is clear (if all the girls are dancing) that there are more boys. On the other hand, if we see some girls sadly watching their friends dancing, it is clear (if all the boys are dancing) that there are more girls.

In these examples we proceeded as follows: we tried to establish a one-to-one correspondence between one set, the first, and part of another set, the second. If this worked out, then the second set had more elements than the first. By employing this method we could prove, for example, that there are fewer fish in the ocean than atoms on the Earth (although both these sets are finite, it is hardly possible to count them). We can do this by simply letting each fish correspond to one of the atoms constituting its body. This sets up a one-to-one correspondence between the set of all fish and part of the set of all atoms on Earth.

Unfortunately, this simple procedure fails to hold good for infinite sets. Indeed, we recently saw that a set can have as many elements as one of its parts. So we are in no position to conclude from the sole fact that A has as many elements as a part of set B, that set A has fewer elements than B.

We shall be more modest in our demands and say that if we can set up a one-to-one correspondence between set A and part of set B, then set B has *no fewer elements than set A*. We could prove that this relation possesses all the fundamental properties of inequalities:

(1) Each set A has no fewer elements than itself.

(2) If set A has no fewer elements than set B, and B has no fewer elements than set C, then A has no fewer elements than C.

(3) If A has no fewer elements than B, and B has no fewer elements than A, then they have equally many elements (that is, we can set up a one-to-one correspondence between the elements of these sets).

The first property follows from the fact that by associating with an element of A that very element we obtain is a one-to-one mapping of A onto itself. The second property is also clear: if A can be mapped in a one-to-one manner onto a part of B, and B can be mapped in a one-to-one manner onto a part of C, then A can be mapped in a one-to-one manner onto a part of C.

In spite of its apparent simplicity, the third assertion is fairly difficult to prove. Cantor thought that it was true but for many years was unable to find a proof. In 1897 he lectured at the university of Halle on set theory and mentioned this difficulty. A few days later, one of the students, 19-year-old Felix Bernstein,[8] brought Cantor a proof based on the very same idea the director of the cosmic hotel used to accommodate new guests. Hence this assertion is now called the Cantor-Bernstein theorem. Many years later a proof of this theorem dating back to 1887 was found in the Nachlass of the German mathematician Dedekind.

We will now explain what we mean when we say that the cardinality of a set B is greater than the cardinality of a set A.

It can happen that set B has no fewer elements than set A, but these sets are not equivalent. In other words, there could exist a one-to-one correspondence between set A and part B_1 of set B without there existing a one-to-one correspondence between A and all of set B. This is the case in which we shall say that B has more elements than A.

The countable set – the smallest of the infinite sets. We already said that any infinite subset of the set of natural numbers is countable. Let us now prove that any infinite set contains a countable subset. We can conclude from this that the cardinality of a countable set is not greater than the cardinality of any infinite set, i.e., that this cardinality is the smallest infinite cardinality.

We can select a countable subset from an infinite set A in the following way: Take any element x_1 – we can do this because the set A is infinite, and so is certainly not empty. Clearly, we have not exhausted the elements of A with the selection of element x_1, so that we can proceed to select a second element x_2. After that, we choose a third element x_3, etc. We have thus extracted from set A a countable subset X of indexed elements:

$$X = \{x_1, x_2, \ldots, x_n, \ldots\}.$$

By making a slight change in the argument we can arrange matters so that an infinite set will be left even after the extraction of the countable subset. All we have to do is put back into A all those elements from X that have even indices. After doing this, we have extracted a countable subset

$$Y = \{x_1, x_3, x_5, \ldots\}$$

and the remaining part of the set still contains an infinite subset of elements: $\{x_2, x_4, x_6, \ldots, x_{2n}, \ldots\}$ (and possibly other elements).

It is not difficult to prove the following theorems.

The cardinality of an infinite set is not changed when we adjoin a countable set to it.

The cardinality of an uncountable set is not changed when we extract a countable subset from it.

These theorems again assert that countable sets are the smallest infinite sets.

Uncountable sets. All the sets we have constructed so far have been countable. This naturally leads us to ask whether all infinite sets are countable. If so, the mathematician would have an easy life: all infinite sets would have equally many elements and no further analysis of infinity would be necessary. But the situation turns out to be more complicated than that; uncountable sets exist, and of more than one cardinality. We are already acquainted with one uncountable set – the set of all points on a straight line. But rather than speak of this set, we are going to discuss a set closely related to it, the set A of ways in which the rooms of the extraordinary hotel can be occupied.

Note that it is usually not easy to prove that a set is uncountable. After all, to prove that a set is countable means simply to invent a method of enumerating its elements. But to prove that a set is uncountable we have to prove that no such method exists. In other words, no matter what method we applied, some element of the set would fail to be counted. Cantor conceived of a very clever method for proving the uncountability of sets which is called the diagonal process. Cantor's method of proof is made clear by the following story about Ion the Quiet.

The census that never took place. Up to now I have talked about the successes of the director of the extraordinary hotel: about how he managed to find places for an infinite set of new guests in his already full hotel, and how he later was able to find places even for the guests from infinitely many such unusual hotels. But there was a time when even this wizard met failure.

An order came down from the commissioner of cosmic hotels to compile a list as quickly as possible of all the possible ways in which the rooms of the hotel could be occupied. The list was to be presented in the form of a table, each line of which was to reflect one of the various ways of occupying the hotel. The filled rooms were to be indicated by ones and the empty rooms by zeros. For example, the sequence

$$101010101010\ldots$$

meant that all the odd rooms were filled and all the even rooms were empty. The sequence

$$11111111111\ldots$$

meant that the entire hotel was filled, while the sequence

$$00000000000\ldots$$

indicated a financial catastrophe – all the rooms were empty.

The director was overloaded with work and therefore conceived of a simple way out of the situation. He charged the man on duty on each floor to compose a list of the ways in which just the rooms in his charge could be occupied. No two ways on the list were to be the same. After a few days the lists were presented to the director and he combined them all into one list.

"Are you sure that this list is complete?" I asked the director. "Isn't there some other way of occupying the rooms?"

"I don't know" he replied. "There are infinitely many ways listed and I don't know how to test the list for completeness."

At this point an idea flashed into my head (by the way, I may be overestimating my talents, because not all traces of my discussions with Professor Tarantog on infinite sets had vanished from my mind).

"I can guarantee that the list is incomplete. I can select a way that is sure to be lacking."

"I agree that the list is probably incomplete. But you won't succeed in selecting a way that isn't listed; after all, there are already infinitely many listed."

We made a bet. I proposed to win it by nailing each sequence on the door of the room to which it corresponded (the reader will recall that there were just as many ways listed as rooms in the hotel). I then proceeded in a very simple fashion. Going up to the door of the first room, I saw that the corresponding sequence started with the digit 0. The digit 1 quickly appeared on my writing pad; this was the first digit of the sequence I wanted to construct.

When I went up to the door of the second room, I wasn't interested in the first digit of the sequence; after all, I already had the first digit of my sequence. So I directed my attention to the second digit. Seeing that this was 1, I wrote the digit 0 on my pad. Similarly, when I noticed that the third digit of the sequence nailed to the third room was also 1, I again wrote the digit 0 on my pad. In general, when I found that the nth digit of the nth sequence was 0, then I wrote the digit 1 in the nth place on my pad, but if the nth digit of the nth sequence was 1, then I wrote 0.

After I had gone past all the rooms of the hotel[*] a sequence of zeros and ones had been written on my pad.

Going to the director's office, I said:

"Here, feast your eyes on the missing sequence."
"And how do you know that it's lacking?"
"It can't be the first because it has a different first digit. It can't be the second because it has a different second digit; in general, it can't be the nth because it has a different nth digit."

The bet was won, and I gained the privilege of staying at the hotel whenever I wanted at no charge.

But it at once became clear that no matter what countable set of sequences you took, there would always be a sequence that didn't appear in the list (you would always be able to hang them on the doors of the rooms). This means that the set of all ways of occupying the hotel is uncountable, and the task given the director was not one that could be carried out.

We decided to send a telegram describing the situation. I should point out that the telegraph in use at the extraordinary hotel was itself unusual: it could send telegrams composed of an infinite set (more precisely, a countable set) of

---

[*]Hm, how much time did he have to spend?

dots and dashes. For example, the telegram might have the form

$$-.--.---.etc.$$

I quickly grasped the fact that the set of all such telegrams was also uncountable; after all, you could just as well put zeros and ones in place of the dots and dashes, and then there would be no difference at all between the telegrams with a countable set of signs and the set of all ways of occupying the hotel.

After sending the telegram, I took leave of the director of the hotel and took off for galaxy RGC-8067, where I was to carry out an astrographical survey.

The uncountability of the continuum. Now it will not be difficult to prove that the set of all points on a line is uncountable. In place of it we can discuss the set of all real numbers, since to each point on the line there corresponds a real number, and conversely.

Any real number can be given an infinite decimal expansion of the form

$$a.\alpha_1\alpha_2\alpha_3\ldots\alpha_n\ldots$$

Some even have two expansions, for example: $0.500\ldots$ and $0.49999\ldots$ represent the same number. To simplify matters we shall employ the expansion with the zeros.

Suppose that by some scheme we had managed to enumerate all the real numbers. In order to show that this can't happen we need only show that some number has not been enumerated. Following in Ion the Quiet's footsteps, we proceed in the following manner.

We first write zero followed by a decimal point. We then take the first number in our enumeration and examine its first place after the decimal point (i.e., its tenths place). If it differs from 1, then we write a 1 after the decimal point in the number we are constructing; but if it is 1, we put a 2 after the decimal point. After that we choose the second number in our enumeration and examine its second place after the decimal point. Again, if this number is different from 1, we put the number 1 in the hundredths place in our number; and if it is 1, then we use 2. We carry on in this way, each time looking at the nth place in the nth number of our enumeration. As a result of these operations we get some number, for example:

$$N = 0.1121211\ldots$$

It is clear that this number is not one of those enumerated: it differs from the first number in the first decimal place; it differs from the second number in the second decimal place; it differs from the nth number in the nth decimal place, etc.

In order to make it clearer to the reader how we determine our number different from all those enumerated, suppose that in the given enumeration the first five numbers have the following form:

$$4.27364\ldots$$
$$-1.31225\ldots$$
$$7.95471\ldots$$
$$0.62419\ldots$$
$$8.56280\ldots$$

Then the number not in the enumeration will begin with the following decimals:

$$0.12121\ldots$$

Naturally, this is not the only number that is not on the list (we could have replaced all the decimals except 2 by 2 and replaced 2 by 7, or chosen some other rule). But we only needed to establish the existence of a single number which does not appear in the enumeration in order to demonstrate that the supposed enumeration of all the real numbers could not exist.

The existence of transcendental numbers. Numbers are called *transcendental numbers* if they are not the roots of any equation with integer coefficients of the form

$$a_0 x^n + a_1 x^{n-1} + \cdots + a_n = 0.$$

As we saw, the numbers which *are* roots of such equations are called *algebraic numbers*.

During a long period in its history, mathematics only dealt with algebraic numbers, such as $7/15$, $\sqrt[8]{10}$, $\sqrt{2} + \sqrt[3]{3}$, etc. It was only at the cost of a great effort that, in 1844, the French mathematician Liouville[9] was able to find a few transcendental numbers. But the proof that the number π is transcendental, carried out by Lindemann[10] in 1882, was a great mathematical event; indeed, it followed that it is impossible to square the circle. And suddenly it became clear that the algebraic numbers met with at every step in mathematics are really extremely rare, while the transcendental numbers, so hard to construct, are really the common ones. After all, we have already seen that the algebraic numbers only form a countable set; while the set of all real numbers, as we just demonstrated, is uncountable. This means that the real numbers which are not algebraic, i.e., the transcendental numbers, must also be uncountable.

This proof of the existence of transcendental numbers, obtained by Cantor in 1873, differed from Liouville's proof in that it used only the notions of countability and uncountability of sets and not special properties of algebraic numbers. Liouville's theorem implies that the number $0.1010010000001\ldots$, in whose decimal expansion the n-th 1 is followed by $n!$ zeros, is transcendental. To obtain an example of a transcendental number through Cantor's proof one must follow a far longer road: first enumerate the algebraic numbers, then write them in decimal form, then use the diagonal procedure to obtain a transcendental number. It would take a "practical infinity" to find, say, the 10^{100}-th digit in the decimal expansion of this number. On the other hand, Liouville's method enables us to form transcendental numbers for which one can, admittedly with difficulty, answer such questions. Thus the downside of the general method of proof is its relative uselessness in dealing with concrete questions.

Long and short line segments have equally many points. If the reader had been unacquainted with the remarkable properties of infinite sets, the question "Are there more points on a line segment 1 foot long or on a line segment 1 mile long?" would hardly have raised a shadow of doubt in his mind. The answer would be clear; there are many more points on the segment of length 1 mile, for isn't it 5280 times longer? But by now the reader has probably learned to beware of making categorical statements – the properties of infinite sets are too dissimilar to what he has been taught to expect by daily life.

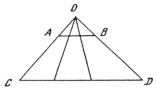

Figure 8.

And the long and short segments do in fact have equally many points! In other words, it is possible to set up a one-to-one correspondence between the points of these segments. Figure 8 shows the easiest way of doing this.

It is hard to reconcile oneself to the thought that a path a million light years long has only as many points as the radius of an atomic nucleus!

But even more unexpected is the result that there are not even more points on the entire infinite line than on a segment, i.e., a one-to-one correspondence can be set up between the set of points on the line and the set of points on the segment.

We do not even need the whole segment, but can discard its endpoints (i.e., we use the open interval). It is clear from Figure 9 how to set up a one-to-one correspondence between the interval AB and the line. Clearly, each point on the interval corresponds to exactly one point on the line and every point on the line has a partner on the interval.

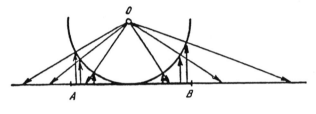

Figure 9

However, this correspondence can be set up in another way with the help of a curve – the tangent curve, the graph of the function $y = \tan x$ (Figure 10).

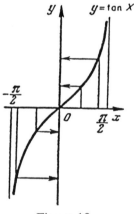

Figure 10

Segment and square. Mathematicians reluctantly reconciled themselves to the fact that there are as many points on a segment as on an infinite line. But the following result of Cantor turned out to be even more unexpected. Searching for a set which would have more points than a segment, he turned to the set of points of a square. He had no doubt of the result – after all, the segment occupied only one side of the square, whereas the set of all segments which composed the square had the cardinality of the continuum.

Cantor searched for three years (from 1871 to 1874) for a proof that it was impossible to set up a one-to-one correspondence between the points of the segment and the points of the square.

The years went by, but the desired result could not be obtained. And then the completely unexpected happened. He succeeded in setting up the correspondence he believed impossible! He wrote to the mathematician Dedekind: "I see it, but I don't believe it."

But we have to resign ourselves to the fact that our intuition lets us down again here – it turns out that there are exactly as many points in the square as on the segment. A rigorous proof of the statement is made somewhat complicated by the lack of uniqueness of the decimal expansion of numbers. We shall therefore present only a sketch of Cantor's proof.

Let us take the segment [0,1] and the square of side 1. We may suppose that the square is situated as in Figure 11. We have to set up a one-to-one correspondence between the points of the segment and the points of the square. Projection of the points of the square onto the segment AB will not help here; indeed, under projection an infinite set of points of the square are sent into one point of the segment (for example, all the points of segment DA go into point A).

We can solve the problem as follows: We can specify any point T of the square $ABCD$ by means of two numbers, its coordinates x and y (or more simply its distances along the sides AB and AD). These numbers can be written as infinite decimals. Since x and y are not

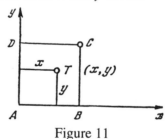

Figure 11

more than 1, these decimals have the form

$$x = 0.\alpha_1\alpha_2 \ldots \alpha_n \ldots \qquad (2.2)$$

$$y = 0.\beta_1\beta_2 \ldots \beta_n \ldots \qquad (2.3)$$

(for the sake of simplicity we do not take points lying on the sides of the square, but only take interior points). For example, if $x = 0.63205 \ldots$ and $y =$

$0.21357\ldots$, then $\alpha_1 = 6$, $\alpha_2 = 3$, $\alpha_3 = 2$, etc., and $\beta_1 = 2$, $\beta_2 = 1$, $\beta_3 = 3$, etc.

Now we have to pick the point Q of the segment AB which is to correspond to T. It is enough to say what the length of the segment AQ is. We choose this length to be equal to the number z, whose decimal expansion is obtained by interlacing the decimal expansions of x and y. In other words, we form a third expansion from the two expansions (2) and (3) by combining their decimals:

$$z = 0.\alpha_1\beta_1\alpha_2\beta_2\alpha_3\beta_3\ldots\alpha_n\beta_n\ldots$$

For instance, if

$$x = 0.515623\ldots$$

and

$$y = 0.734856\ldots$$

then we obtain

$$z = 0.571354682536\ldots$$

The point z lies on the segment $[0,1]$, and it is clear that different points of the square correspond to different points of the segment. Indeed, if points T and T' are not the same, then the decimal expansion of x and x' or y and y' must differ at least in one place. But this will lead to a difference in the decimal expansions of the numbers z and z'. A somewhat more detailed analysis shows that, conversely, the points corresponding to two different decimal expansions also do not coincide.

Thus we have set up a one-to-one correspondence between the points of the square and the points of a part of the segment $[0,1]$. This shows that the set of points of the square has a cardinality no larger than that of the set of points of the segment. But its cardinality is certainly no smaller, so that the cardinalities must coincide.

Not just the square, but the cube as well has only as many points as the segment. In general, any geometric figure containing at least one line segment will have just as many points as the segment. Such sets are called sets with the cardinality of the *continuum* (from the Latin *continuum* – unbroken).

Is there a set of largest cardinality? Till now the largest cardinality we have become acquainted with is that of the set of points on the line, i.e., the cardinality of the continuum. Neither the set of points of the square nor the set of points of the cube has a larger cardinality. Perhaps the cardinality of the continuum is the largest possible? This turns out not to be the case. Indeed, there is *no* set of largest cardinality. Given any set A, there is a set B of cardinality greater than the cardinality of A. We can construct it by first associating with each point a of a set A the function assuming the value 1 at this point and the value 0 at the remaining points. Clearly, distinct points give rise to distinct functions. For example, if set A consists of the points 1,2,3, then point 1 corresponds to a function which assumes the value 1 at this point, while point 2 corresponds to a function assuming the value 0 at point 1. These functions are distinct. We take our set B to be the set of all functions on A with values 0 and 1.

Thus, the cardinality of set B is not less than the cardinality of set A. Let us now show that these cardinalities are not equal, i.e., no one-to-one correspondence can be found between the elements of sets A and B. Indeed, suppose such a correspondence existed.

We designate the function corresponding to element a of A by $f_a(x)$. Remember that all the functions $f_a(x)$ assume only the two values 0 and 1.

Let us define a new function $\varphi(x)$ by means of the equation:

$$\varphi(x) = 1 - f_x(x). \tag{2.3}$$

Thus, in order to determine the value of the function $\varphi(x)$ at some point a of A we first must find the function $f_a(x)$ corresponding to this point and subtract its value at $x = a$ from 1. It is now clear that the function $\varphi(x)$ is defined on the set A and assumes only the values 0 and 1. Consequently, $\varphi(x)$ is an element of set B. But then by our assumption $\varphi(x)$ corresponds to some point b of A; this means that

$$\varphi(x) = f_b(x). \tag{2.4}$$

It follows from (3) and (4) that for all x in A

$$1 - f_x(x) = f_b(x).$$

Let us set $x = b$ in this equation. Then we get

$$1 - f_b(b) = f_b(b)$$

so that

$$f_b(b) = \frac{1}{2}.$$

But this contradicts the requirement that the values of the function $f_b(x)$ be 0 and 1. The contradiction we have obtained shows that there can be no one-to-one correspondence between sets A and B.

Thus, given any set A, we can construct a set B of larger cardinality. Therefore, no set of largest cardinality can exist. Beginning with the smallest infinite cardinality – that of the set of natural numbers, we obtain first the cardinality of the continuum, then the cardinality of the set of functions on the set of real numbers, and continue to ascend the dizzying staircase of ever increasing infinite cardinalities.

The arithmetic of the infinite. The arithmetic of natural numbers is not just counting "one, two, three." We can add and multiply natural numbers and raise a natural number to a power. There is a close connection between these operations and operations on finite sets. When adding natural numbers m and n we are computing the number of elements in the union of two *disjoint* sets with m and n elements respectively. When multiplying m by n we are computing the number of pairs (a, b), where the first element belongs to a set A with m elements, and the second to a set B with n elements. In mathematics this set of pairs is called the *Cartesian product* of the sets A and B and is denoted by $A \times B$.

Denote the union of disjoint sets A and B by $A + B$ and the cardinality of A by $|A|$. Then what we just said can be written as follows:

$$|A + B| = |A| + |B|$$
$$|A \times B| = |A||B|.$$

The left-hand sides of these equalities make sense for infinite sets. This allows us to define addition and multiplication of infinite cardinalities. Denote by $\mathbb{N}$ the set of natural numbers and by Δ the set of points of the interval [0,1]. Then our earlier results on cardinalities can be written as follows:

$$n + |\mathbb{N}| = |\mathbb{N}|, |\mathbb{N}| + |\mathbb{N}| = |\mathbb{N}|, |\mathbb{N}||\mathbb{N}| = |\mathbb{N}|, |\mathbb{N}| + |\Delta| = |\Delta|, |\mathbb{N}||\Delta| = |\Delta|,$$
$$|\Delta||\Delta| = |\Delta|,$$

and so on. For example, the equality $|\mathbb{N}||\mathbb{N}| = |\mathbb{N}|$ states that the union of a countable set of countable sets is countable, and the equality $|\Delta||\Delta| = |\Delta|$ states that a square has as many points as a segment.

It is not difficult to prove that for *finite* sets A and B the number of all mappings with domain A and range in B is $|B|^{|A|}$. It is therefore reasonable to define $|B|^{|A|}$, for sets A and B with *arbitrary* cardinalities $|A|$ and $|B|$, as the cardinality of the set of mappings with domain A and range in B. For example, $2^{|\mathbb{N}|} = |\Delta|$ states that the cardinality of the set of sequences of zeros and ones is the same as the cardinality of the continuum.

We can now understand what Cantor had in mind when he said that the laws of arithmetic of the infinite differ radically from those of the realm of the finite.

Transfinite numbers. Natural numbers are used not only to answer the question of "how many?" but also, in the case of an ordered set, the question "in which place is it?" Thus the natural numbers are used as *quantitative numbers* as well as *ordinal numbers*. Cardinalities can be used only as quantitative numbers. To describe order we must use other concepts. After all, the simplest infinite set, namely the set $\mathbb{N}$ of natural numbers, can be ordered in infinitely many ways. In addition to the usual ordering 1,2,3,4,5,6,... we can start with the odd numbers (in their usual order) and then set down the even numbers (also in their usual order): 1,3,5,...,2,4,6,.... If we try to enumerate the natural numbers in this ordering then we get into trouble – all numbers will have been used to enumerate the odd numbers and it will be necessary to introduce additional symbols. To deal with this case, Cantor suggested the label ω for 2, $\omega + 1$ for 4, and so on.

Even more symbols are needed if we take first all numbers divisible by 3, then those which leave the remainder 1 when divided by 3, and then those that leave the remainder 2 upon division by 3: 3,6,9,...,1,4,7,...,2,5,8,.... Here 2 is labelled $\omega \cdot 2$, 5 is labelled $\omega \cdot 2 + 1$, and so on. And if we order the natural numbers by writing first the primes, then products of two primes, then products of three primes, and so on, and at the very end the number 1 (which is neither prime nor composite), it will have to be labelled with the new symbol ω^ω.

Cantor thought up many other orderings of the natural numbers. They all share (with the orderings just introduced) the property that every subset of the natural numbers has in each of these orderings a least element. Cantor called (possibly uncountable) ordered sets with the corresponding property *well-ordered*, and the symbols he introduced for their indexing *transfinite numbers* or *transfinite ordinals* (*trans* is Latin for beyond). In the study of transfinite numbers Cantor encountered the problem of the cardinality of the set of *countable* transfinite numbers. It is easy to show that this cardinality is uncountable and not greater than the cardinality of the continuum. But neither Cantor, nor his many students and followers could say whether it is equal to or less than the cardinality of the continuum. We will discuss the present state of this co-called *continuum problem* in Chapter 4.

At the beginning of the 20th century the theory of infinite sets became a fashionable area of mathematics. Some experts attached very great importance to investigations in this area. For example, A. Fraenkel wrote:

> The conquest of the actual infinite by means of set theory can be regarded as an extension of our scientific horizon whose importance is comparable to the importance of the Copernican system in astronomy and the theory of relativity and quantum mechanics in physics.

But in the end, time, the harshest of all judges, puts everything in its proper perspective. The number of papers in which the authors used transfinite numbers or investigated cardinalities beyond the countable and beyond the cardinality of the continuum decreased steadily. Sets with such cardinalities can be obtained by considering all subsets of the plane or all functions on [0,1]. But the fact is that virtually all theoretical investigations and the solution of practical problems involve not arbitrary subsets of the plane and arbitrary functions but those obtained by certain definite processes from very simple ones. And sets of such "good" subsets and functions have the cardinality of the continuum.

In spite of the view of P.S. Aleksandrov[11] and A.N. Kolmogorov[12] that "the tremendous influence of set theory on the evolution of mathematics in the last half-century is at present a universally conceded fact," this influence moves at present in very different channels. In the next chapter we will describe the changes in certain areas of mathematics due to set-theoretic conceptions.

Chapter 3

Remarkable functions and curves, or a stroll through a mathematical hall of wonders

General foundation. The whole history of the evolution of mathematics is marked by dialectical opposition and unity of its two parts devoted to the study of numbers and figures, respectively. The natural numbers differ from one another by their properties: some are even and some odd, some are prime and some composite, some can be written as sums of two squares and some can not. This infinite variety of properties that change so strikingly upon addition of just one unit to a number endows number theory with a special charm. Of course, geometric figures are just as varied – triangles and squares, circles and parabolas, astroids and cardioids. But each curve by itself, a straight line or a circle, is composed of points with identical properties.

The idea of the infinite also takes different forms in these two branches of mathematics. In arithmetic it is embodied in the sequence of natural numbers, while in geometry it appears in the infinity of space and, at the same time, in the infinite divisibility of figures. And yet, notwithstanding this seemingly unbridgeable chasm – due perhaps to some profound characteristics of human reason – throughout the history of mathematics there have been endless attempts to link arithmetic and geometry and to derive all of mathematics from a single foundation.

When mathematics was not so much a science as a trade plied by Egyptian and Babylonian scribes, the unity of arithmetic and geometry manifested itself in naive form– the many problems dealt with included computations of areas of figures and of volumes of solids. The first attempt to effect a theoretical unification of arithmetic and geometry was undertaken in the sixth century BC in the school of the ancient Greek mathematician and philosopher Pythagoras.

One of Pythagoras' pronouncements that has come down to us is "All is number." He not only tried to "verify harmony by means of algebra" by creating one of the first mathematical theories of the musical scale, but also attempted to base the science of measurement of geometric magnitudes on the natural numbers. That is why the discovery of the incommensurability of the side and diagonal of a square by a Pythagorean spelled a catastrophe for the Pythagorean worldview. (For a long time this discovery was withheld from the uninitiated.)

When it became clear that geometry could not be based on the concept of natural number, the ancient Greek mathematicians adopted the opposite approach and began to express relations between arbitrary magnitudes in geometric terms. Whereas the discrete lent itself more readily to logical analysis, the continuous could be more readily grasped by intuition. Relying on geometric language, Greek scholars stated algebraic laws (this was when terms such as *square* and *cube of a number*, *geometric mean*, and *geometric progression* first entered mathematics), investigated quadratic irrationalities, and solved cubic equations. Geometry itself they based on the idea of the infinite divisibility of lines, (plane) figures, and solids. They created the concepts of a dimensionless point, of a line that had only length, and of a geometric surface without thickness. And in spite of the fact that these were just bold abstractions from real points, lines and surfaces, they served their inventors well in their investigations and enabled them to obtain correct formulas for areas and volumes.

After the fall of antique civilization, the center of mathematical investigations shifted to Arabic-speaking countries. Arabic scholars were familiar not only with the ancient Greek heritage but also with the tradition, derived from Babylonian scribes, that included general methods of solution of arithmetical problems. They were also influenced by the discoveries of Indian mathematicians, who constructed the decimal number system and, unlike the ancient Greek scholars, made free use of negative numbers. All this prepared the ground for the creation of algebra, which first came into being in the 9th century as the art of solving equations. At that time, mathematicians, many of whom lived in Central Asia, paid little attention to subtleties connected with incommensurable segments and freely used numbers in the study of geometric problems.

In Western Europe, the study of algebra began a few centuries later. Italy was the first center of such studies. Western European mathematicians obtained formulas for the solution of cubic and quartic equations, began the study of complex numbers, and developed literal symbolism. At first, in accordance with ancient Greek traditions, literal calculus was geometric in form, and this blocked the use of expressions involving different powers.

Mathematics was faced with the need to construct algebra without reliance on geometric concepts and to free it from an essentially extrinsic geometric terminology. A decisive step in this direction was taken by Descartes.[1] At first sight there seemed to be nothing special in his approach. He suggested that a segment *e* be fixed and called a *unit segment*. But this meant that a product of two segments *a* and *b* could be regarded not as the area of a rectangle with sides *a* and *b* but as the length of a segment *c* such that $a : e = c : b$ (we note that the theory of proportions had been worked out in great detail by the ancient Greek scholars). The square root of *a* was interpreted as the geometric mean of the segments *a* and *e*. After Descartes, mathematicians could freely use arbitrary algebraic expressions without worrying about their geometric sense. Descartes' works initiated a period of "arithmetization" of mathematics that lasted more than two hundred years. This process replaced its geometric foundation with an arithmetic one.

A high point of this development was the nongeometric construction of the real numbers. This was done in the 1870s by Cantor, Weierstrass,[2] Dedekind and Méray.[3] The starting point of their definitions was the concept of a natural number. After Descartes, mathematicians could describe geometric objects by means of real numbers (for example, a point by its coordinates). This made possible the "arithmetization" of geometry. The result was a new unity of mathematics based on an arithmetical foundation. At that time, scholars believed that they had reduced the continuous to the discrete.

It was no accident that one of the creators of the arithmetical construction of the real numbers was Cantor, the creator of set theory, another his teacher and inspirer Weierstrass, and the third Dedekind, who in his works came very close to the ideas of set theory. While their constructions were different, each of them defined a real number in terms of an infinite set of rational numbers. For example, in Weierstrass' theory, a real number was defined as an infinite decimal. To give such an infinite decimal one had to specify ten subsets of the natural numbers, each of which specified the locations of a particular digit. In Dedekind's theory, a real number α was defined by simply subdividing the rationals into two subsets, one of which contained the numbers not exceeding α, and the other the numbers greater than α.

At the same time Gottlob Frege[4] tried to base the arithmetic of natural numbers on the set concept. This made the theory of infinite sets the common foundation of arithmetic and geometry, of the discrete and the continuous. It seemed that first one must master infinite sets, then set aside in their theory a tiny corner where finite sets would humbly huddle together, and only then obtain the natural numbers. In Hilbert's[5] words,

> owing to the gigantic simultaneous efforts of Frege, Dedekind and Cantor, the infinite was set on a throne and revelled in its total triumph. In its daring flight the infinite reached dizzying heights of success.

But not all scholars accepted without demur the new view of mathematics. At first, Cantor's discoveries were received with disbelief and even outright antagonism by many mathematicians and with indifference by an overwhelming majority of philosophers. The leader of the opposition against the new view was Kronecker,[6] one of the most eminent mathematicians of that time. His key tenet was that mathematics can deal only with what is built up out of natural numbers in finitely many steps. His famous motto was that "God created the natural numbers and all the rest is the work of man." He therefore rejected not only the theory of infinite sets, generally regarded as extravagant, but also the newfangled theory of real numbers.

The unenthusiastic reception accorded Cantor's work by many mathematicians can in part be explained by the fact that the very idea of regarding the infinite as something completed contradicted the established views. Consequently, many scholars viewed research in the area of infinite sets as something far from the vital tasks of science. In part, this unhappy state of affairs was due to Cantor's style – a medley of mathematical investigations with philosophical and theological digressions. Transfinite numbers met with a guarded reception because they could not be used to evaluate a complicated integral, sum a difficult series, or solve a differential equation. And Cantor's successes in the realm of concrete mathematics (for example, his proof of the existence of transcendental numbers) seemed rather unimpressive.

But there was one area of mathematics in which set theory was something like daily bread. This was the then ultramodern theory of functions of a real variable. To understand why Cantor's ideas were particularly useful in this area of mathematics, we must recall the course of evolution of the concept of a function.

How the notion of a function developed. The majority of mathematical concepts underwent a long period of development. They first arose as generalizations of intuitive ideas derived from everyday experience. With gradual elimination of details and accidental aspects, these intuitive ideas slowly crystallized into exact mathematical definitions. But it often happened that these

definitions applied not only to those objects whose study led to their formulation, but also to other objects that had not been thought of earlier. The study
of these new objects was begun and the process of abstraction was carried to
ever higher levels; next came the extension of the original definitions on the
basis provided by the studies. Ever broader meaning came to be attributed
to mathematical concepts; they embraced wider and wider classes of objects,
occurring in more varied fields of mathematics.

The notion of a function also followed a tortuous path. The idea of the
interdependence of two quantities apparently arose in classical Greek science,
where it was used in geometry. At the beginning of the 17th century Galileo,
Kepler and other scientists began to develop kinematics, the study of the motion
of bodies. Under the influence of their works, Descartes introduced into mathematics the general notion of a variable magnitude. Here is Engels' evaluation
of this development:

> Descartes' notion of a *variable magnitude* was a watershed in math-
> ematics. Through it *motion*, and thus *dialectic*, entered mathemat-
> ics . . . and *made differential and integral calculus necessary*. In
> fact, the calculus came into being at that time, and, by and large,
> it was completed rather than invented by Newton and Leibniz.

Seventeenth-century scientists used variable magnitudes to describe the
most varied motions. As a result, the geometric language of mathematics
was gradually replaced by the language of mechanics. For example, when he
introduced the logarithmic function into science, Napier[7] relied on rectilinear
motions of points, and Newton felt that mathematical analysis must study the
time dependence of various magnitudes – such as displacements, velocities and
accelerations – that characterize motions. Incidentally, for some time geometric
language was retained. For example, instead of trigonometric functions of a
numerical argument, one studied the lengths of certain segments in a disk as
functions of an angle. In fact, Leibniz first introduced the very notion of a
function as a connection between certain segments characterizing points on a
curve (abscissas and ordinates, abscissas and subtangents, and so on).

But in 1718, J. Bernoulli[8] gave the following definition of a function free
of geometric imagery:

> A function of a variable quantity is a magnitude formed in some
> manner from this variable quantity and constants

and Euler[9] defined a function as follows:

Quantities dependent on others such that as the second change, so
do the first, are said to be functions.

Also, Euler managed to free trigonometry of geometric language and to
introduce trigonometric functions as functions of numerical variables.

In Euler's time it was thought that a function must be expressed by means
of a single formula, so a relation not so expressible was regarded as "sewn
together" from functions. For example, the relation

$$y = \begin{cases} x, & \text{if } x < 0 \\ x^2, & \text{if } x \geq 0, \end{cases}$$

was thought to consist of *two different* functions.

It soon became clear that the matter was significantly more complex. When
he solved the problem of the vibrating string, D. Bernoulli[10] obtained an answer
in the form of an infinite series whose terms were products of two trigonometric
functions, one of the moment t in time and the other of the coordinate of the point
of the string. According to the then accepted view, this meant that the deflection
of the string was a function of two variables given by a single expression.

This same problem of the vibrating string was solved by D'Alembert.
D'Alembert's solution had a form quite different from Bernoulli's, and, what
is most important, could be given by different formulas for different values of
the argument.

What looked to be an insoluble contradiction now loomed up before 18th-
century mathematics: two answers had been obtained for the same problem,
one expressed by a single formula for all values of the argument and another
by several formulas. D. Bernoulli's solution was questioned because it was
thought that he had not found all solutions to the problem, just the solutions
expressible in a single formula. A bitter controversy arose in which all the
prominent mathematicians of the 18th century – Euler, d'Alembert, and others
– took part.

The controversy, in essence, was over the concept of a function, the connection between functional dependence and the possibility of expressing this
dependence by means of a formula. A definitive solution to the question was
obtained at the beginning of the 19th century, when the French mathematician
J. Fourier[11] showed that the sum of an infinite series of trigonometric functions
can be expressed by different formulas over different intervals. He then gave a
new definition of function, stressing that the main thing was the assignment of
values for the function; whether this assignment was carried out by means of a
single formula or not was unimportant.

Fourier's result was refined by the German mathematician Dirichlet, who showed that any given curve can be the graph of the sum of a trigonometric series. It is required only that the number of maxima and minima on the curve be finite and the curve be bounded in amplitude.

After a long debate that involved many eminent scholars (including Lobachevski) the following definition of function was universally accepted:

> A variable quantity y is said to be a function of a variable quantity x, if to each value of the quantity x there corresponds a uniquely determined value of the quantity y.

In this definition not a word is said about the function having to be given by a single formula throughout its interval of definition. From the modern standpoint, the only possible flaw of this definition is that it mentions variable magnitudes. From the viewpoint of "pure mathematics" this term is not precisely defined. At the beginning of the 19th century scholars just gave examples of variable magnitudes encountered in physics (temperature of a cooling body, displacement or velocity of nonuniform motion, and so on). They thought that one can associate with each of these variable magnitudes a mathematical variable whose variation described the manner of variation of the physical magnitude. But then one of the most fundamental concepts of mathematics seemed to depend on the physical notion of time.

The creation of the theory of real numbers and of set theory in the second half of the 19th century made possible, among other things, the rigorization of the vague concept of a variable magnitude. It turned out that one should think of a variable as a letter for which one can substitute numbers belonging to some number set X. Of course, this approach to the concept of a variable was more static than the concept accepted by scholars at the beginning of the 19th century. It lacked the sense of motion and variability. But it made possible a definition of function free from extramathematical concepts:

> A function f defined on a number set X is a correspondence rule that associates with every x in X a number $f(x)$.

In this very general formulation, the notion of a function merges with those of *correspondence*, mapping, transformation, operator, and so on.

For example, from this point of view the area of a triangle is a function defined on the set of all triangles and assuming its values in the set of positive numbers. And the circle inscribed in a triangle is a function defined on the set of all triangles with values in the set of circles. In view of the fact, that in a coordinatized plane, triangles and circles are determined by certain sets of numbers, these functions can be reduced to numerical functions. In general, numerical functions are one of the most important kinds of functions. That is why, in the sequel, we will restrict ourselves to functions defined on sets of numbers and assuming numerical values.

Under a microscope. The rigorization of mathematical concepts cuts both ways. On the positive side, it eliminates much that is unclear, increases the precision of mathematical discourse, and results in more conclusive proofs. But then there are losses. What science gains in terms of rigor it often pays for with loss of intuitive appeal. Also, there is always the question whether the rigorous definitions correspond to the crude, intuitive images they are supposed to model mathematically. Thus the stumbling blocks removed from the field of mathematics often do not disappear but are merely transferred to the boundary between mathematics and its applications.

But for mathematics precise definitions are a vital necessity. By studying the properties of the concepts determined by these definitions, scholars learn the properties of the mathematical models by means of which they are trying to describe the real world. If the properties of a particular model do not quite live up to expectations, then all this means is that in the process of its construction one left out important aspects of the objects the model was supposed to describe.

Therefore, as soon as they rigorized the notion of a function, mathematicians embarked on its thorough study. Then it turned out that many of the objects covered by the rigorous definition were most unlikely to have been studied by mathematicians of past centuries. For example, Dirichlet observed that the correspondence

$$f(x) = \begin{cases} 0, & \text{if } x \text{ is irrational,} \\ 1, & \text{if } x \text{ is rational} \end{cases}$$

is a function.

No 18th-century mathematician would have studied such a correspondence. They studied only functions that described dependencies between physical or geometric magnitudes. But all measurements of concrete magnitudes involve errors, and for such magnitudes it makes no sense to ask whether their values are rational or irrational. Of course, one can object that the value of the function

$$\text{sgn } x = \begin{cases} -1, & \text{if } x < 0, \\ 0, & \text{if } x = 0, \\ 1, & \text{if } x > 0, \end{cases}$$

is not well determined near the point $x = 0$ – a small error of measurement can change the function value sharply from negative to positive. But 18th-century mathematicians knew that a function like sgn x is a mathematical idealization of a continuous function that grows abruptly in the region around $x = 0$. As for the Dirichlet function, it was useless for the most idealized description of *any* real process.

Even the addition of the requirement of continuity helped little. Using their new freedom, mathematicians began to construct complicated examples of continuous functions that contradicted all the familiar expectations of their predecessors. Henri Poincaré[12] characterized the changed views of scholars at the end of the 19th century concerning the notion of a function in these words: "There was a time when the search for new functions was motivated by some practical aim. Nowadays one invents functions to demonstrate the flaws in the arguments of our predecessors; other than this, no conclusion can be obtained from them." The subsequent evolution of mathematics showed that Poincaré's view was onesided. In modern physics one deals with functions and curves that have very strange properties. But at the end of the 19th century such applications were still in the distant future. Mathematicians delighted in investigating properties of the weirdest functions, which their predecessors would have certainly put in a hall of wonders. Not for nothing did some mathematicians of the classical persuasion refer to the new theory of functions as the "teratology of functions."

Mathematicians at the end of the 19th century seemed to have put functions under a microscope, whereas their predecessors viewed them with the naked eye and could not have discovered the fine features of their "microscopic structure." In theory, 18th-century mathematicians realized that, like all curves, the graphs of functions had no thickness. But when they thought of functions, they imagined their graphs as drawn on a sheet of paper with a pencil, that is as having thickness. *Such* curves are piecewise monotonic, that is they consist of a finite number of pieces that go up or down. Except for a few points, these graphs have tangents everywhere, any two curves in a bounded part of the plane have only finitely many points of intersection, and so on. All this seemed obvious.

These mathematicians did not suspect that there exist functions and curves whose properties do not at all resemble the properties of such "respectable" functions as polynomials, trigonometric and exponential functions, and so on. But the mathematical apparatus they had developed contained the charge of dynamite which subsequently exploded the deceptive state of wellbeing. This dynamite was the theory of infinite series. At first, such series made it easier to compute functional values. But then they became the means of obtaining new functions. And then, in the context of addition of "nice" polynomials, it became clear that adding more and more terms introduced finer and finer "flutters" of the infinite sum-to-be, and in the end one obtained a function with properties very different from those of the functions studied in classical analysis. The behavior of such functions made classical mathematicians think of a madhouse. Thus here too the infinite, the idea of adding infinitely many terms, had a revolutionary effect on the evolution of science.

And now let me invite you on a stroll through a mathematical hall of wonders whose exhibits differ from school displays as much as an ichthyosaur or a dinosaur differs from today's living creatures.

The genie escapes from the bottle. Dirichlet's own function, of which we spoke earlier, was already unusual. After all, there are infinitely many rational and irrational numbers on even the smallest interval of the x axis. But Dirichlet's function is 1 for rational numbers and 0 for irrational numbers. Thus, as we move along the x-axis, the value of the function constantly jumps back and forth between 0 and 1. It is impossible to graph this function, since it is discontinuous at every point.

And even among the continuous functions are some with unexpected properties. For example, can a continuous function have infinitely many maxima and minima on a finite interval? This seems impossible at first glance. After all, the curve has to take up space in falling from a maximum to a minimum, then again rising to a maximum, etc. How can it do all this in a finite interval? Nevertheless, such odd functions do exist and it is quite simple to construct one.

We shall construct such a function on the segment [0,1]. We first cut the segment in two and construct an equilateral triangle on the left half. Now we divide the right half into two equal parts and construct a second equilateral triangle on the segment $[\frac{1}{2}, \frac{3}{4}]$. We carry out the described operation infinitely many times. As a result we find a mountain range with infinitely many peaks gradually dropping down to the point 1 (Figure 12). We take the curve obtained as the graph of the function $f(x)$. Thus, the function is defined at each point of the segment [0, 1] with the exception of the right endpoint 1. Here we put $f(1) = 0$.

Since the height of the peaks approaches 0 as x approaches 1, we obtain a function continuous at all points of the segment [0, 1]. But the number of maxima and minima on this segment is infinite!

In order to construct such a strange function a mathematician of the 18th century would have to spend a lot of time trying out combinations of functions

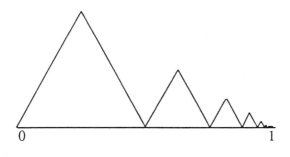

Figure 12

before he would conjecture that the function

$$f(x) = \begin{cases} x \cos \frac{\pi}{x}, & \text{if } x \neq 0 \\ 0, & \text{if } x = 0 \end{cases}$$

has infinitely many maxima and minima on the segment [0,1].

But functions with infinitely many maxima and minima were only the first of the unpleasant surprises in store for mathematicians. The genie had only begun to escape from the bottle.

Wet points. The function we constructed in the preceding section has only one point near which there are infinitely many maxima and minima; this is the point 1. Now we shall construct another function with many more such points.

Imagine that rain is falling on the segment [0, 1] of the x-axis. We go about providing shelter from the rain as follows. We divide the segment [0, 1] into three equal parts and erect a tent in the form of an equilateral triangle in the central part. It protects all the points of the central part from the rain (except the endpoints, i.e., the points $\frac{1}{3}$ and $\frac{2}{3}$).

Now we divide each of the two pieces left over into three parts and protect the central part with a tent of the same form (but only one third as wide). We now have the curve sketched in Figure 13. In the third step of this procedure we erect four more tents, then eight more, etc.

Now we come to the question of whether all the points of the segment have been sheltered by the saw-toothed curve, or whether there remain points wetted by the rain? It is easy to point out some of the "wet" points – these are the endpoints of the sheltered segments (i.e., such points as $\frac{1}{3}$, $\frac{1}{9}$, $\frac{2}{9}$, $\frac{7}{9}$, $\frac{8}{9}$, etc.) All these points were left unprotected when the corresponding tents were erected, and they remain unprotected by the tents erected subsequently. It is

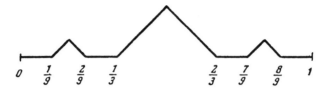

Figure 13

easy to see that there are infinitely many such endpoints, but that they still form only a countable set.

But it turns out that there is an uncountable set of "wet" points in addition to these. It is convenient to use the ternary representation in order to describe them. As we know, the ternary representation is formed in the same way as the decimal representation, except that the numbers are grouped in threes instead of tens. Thus, in the ternary representation we only employ the three digits 0, 1, 2 for writing numbers in place of the ten ordinarily used.

It is easy to learn how to change the representation of a number whose ternary representation is

$$0.02020202\ldots$$

It is represented in the decimal system by the infinite geometric series

$$\frac{2}{3^2} + \frac{2}{3^4} + \frac{2}{3^6} + \cdots$$

The sum of this series is $\frac{1}{4}$. Thus,

$$1/4 = 0.020202\ldots$$

Now we can say exactly which points remain wet after all the protective tents have been set up. The first tent shelters the points lying between $\frac{1}{3}$ and $\frac{2}{3}$. But these are just the points whose ternary representations have the form

$$0.1\ldots$$

where the dots stand for any combination of digits 0, 1, 2 (in the same way that all the points whose decimal representations begin with the digit 1, i.e., have the form $0.1\ldots$, lie between the points $1/10$ and $2/10$).

The points still wet after the first step are those whose ternary representations have the form

$$0.0\ldots$$

or the form
$$0.2\ldots$$

We can prove in the same way that after the two tents of the second step have been set up, the points remaining wet are only those whose ternary representations begin with one of the following four combinations:

$$0.00\ldots$$
$$0.02\ldots$$
$$0.20\ldots$$
$$0.22\ldots$$

Thus, any point in whose ternary representation 1 occurs will at some stage be protected from the rain. In the end only those points remain wet whose ternary representations can be written without using 1. For example, the points

$$1/4 = 0.020202\ldots$$

and

$$3/4 = 0.20202\ldots$$

remain wet.

But now it must be clear why the set of "wet" points has the cardinality of the continuum. After all, this set can be put into one-to-one correspondence with the set of infinite telegrams (see p.61). We can do this by putting a point such as

$$0.20220200\ldots$$

in correspondence with an infinite telegram by replacing 0 by a dot and 2 by a dash. Different numbers correspond to different telegrams when this procedure is followed. We already know that the set of infinite telegrams has the cardinality of the continuum; thus, the set of wet points will also have this cardinality.

The set of points we called wet was first constructed by Cantor, and is now called *Cantor's set*. It is clear from the construction of the tents that there are infinitely many maxima and minima of the saw-toothed curve near each point of Cantor's set.

The Devil's Staircase. There is still another interesting function related to Cantor's set. It is defined as follows. We first divide the segment [0,1] into three equal parts and stipulate that our function equal $\frac{1}{2}$ at each point of the middle third. Then we divide the left and right thirds into three equal parts and

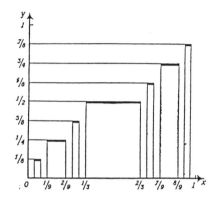

Figure 14

stipulate that the function equal $\frac{1}{4}$ from $\frac{1}{9}$ to $\frac{2}{9}$, and equal $\frac{3}{4}$ from $\frac{7}{9}$ to $\frac{8}{9}$. We now have four segments on which the function is not yet defined:

$$[0, \tfrac{1}{9}] \quad [\tfrac{2}{9}, \tfrac{1}{3}] \quad [\tfrac{2}{3}, \tfrac{7}{9}] \quad [\tfrac{8}{9}, 1]$$

We divide each of these into three equal parts and set the function equal to $\frac{1}{8}$, $\frac{3}{8}, \frac{5}{8}, \frac{7}{8}$, respectively, on the four middle pieces.

Continuing this process, we obtain a function which is defined on all the "dry" points, i.e., on all the points not belonging to Cantor's set. It is easy to define it on the points of this set too, and in such a way that it becomes continuous and nondecreasing on the segment [0,1]. An approximation to the graph of the function obtained is shown in Figure 14. It has the form of a staircase with an infinite number of steps (of course, not all the steps are shown on the graph).

After learning about curves with infinitely many maxima and minima, we are not likely to be surprised at a staircase with an infinite number of steps. But here is something surprising. Let us compute the total length of our staircase. The first step we constructed has length $\frac{1}{3}$, the next two have length $\frac{1}{9}$ apiece, the next four have length $\frac{1}{27}$ apiece, etc. Thus, the sum of the lengths of all the steps is expressed by the infinite geometric series:

$$\frac{1}{3} + \frac{2}{9} + \frac{4}{27} + \dots$$

The sum of this series is

$$\frac{\frac{1}{3}}{1 - \frac{2}{3}} = 1 .$$

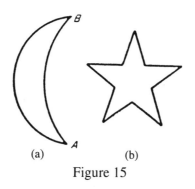

Figure 15

Hence, the total length of the staircase is 1. But the function does not increase at all along these steps; all its rising is concentrated at the points of Cantor's set. But very "few" points fall to the share of this set – even though its cardinality is that of the continuum, its length is zero! (The length of the segment [0,1] is 1 and the total length of the steps is 1.) Thus, our function manages somehow to rise from 0 to 1, even though it only increases on a set of zero length and never makes any jumps! Isn't this really surprising?

A prickly curve. For many centuries mathematicians dealt only with curves at each of whose points a tangent could be constructed. If there were exceptions these occurred at only a few points. The curve seemed to break at these points, and they were therefore called *points of fracture*. The curve drawn in Figure 15a has two *points of fracture*, while the curve drawn in Figure 15b has ten *points of fracture*.

But the curves that we just now constructed already have infinitely many *points of fracture*: the curve associated with Figure 13 has a whole continuum of them. It breaks at each point of the Cantor set and, in addition, at the peaks of all the triangles. However, even the curve associated with Figure 14 has breaks on a comparatively "small" set of points: its length is zero.

For a long time no mathematician believed that there could exist a continuous curve wholly composed of "sawteeth," "breaks," and "prickles." Mathematicians were greatly amazed, therefore, when someone succeeded in constructing such a curve, and what is more, a function with a graph like a picket fence. The first to do this was the Czech mathematician Bolzano. But his work remained unpublished for a long time, and the first published example was that of the German mathematician Weierstrass. However, it is difficult for us to present Weierstrass' example, for it is based on the theory of trigonometric series.

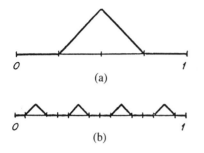

(a)

(b)

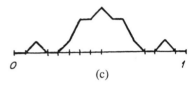

(c)

Figure 16

We shall now discuss Bolzano's example, making a few slight changes. We first divide the segment [0,1] into four equal parts and construct an isosceles right triangle over the two central parts (Figure 16a). The resulting curve is the graph of some function, which we shall denote by $y = f_1(x)$. We next divide each of the four pieces again into four equal parts and correspondingly construct four more isosceles right triangles (Figure 16b). This gives us the graph of a second function $y = f_2(x)$. If we add these two functions, the graph of the sum $y = f_1(x) + f_2(x)$ has the form sketched in Figure 16c. It is clear that this curve already has more breaks and that these breaks are more densely distributed. In the next stage we again divide each piece into four parts, now constructing 16 isosceles right triangles and then adding the corresponding function $y = f_3(x)$ to the function $y = f_1(x) + f_2(x)$.

As we continue this process, we obtain a curve with a larger number of breaks. In the limit we obtain a curve with a break at each point and possessing a tangent at no point.

A similar example of a curve possessing a tangent at no point was constructed by the Swedish mathematician Helge von Koch.[13] He took an equilateral triangle, divided each of its sides into three equal parts, and then constructed new equilateral triangles with peaks pointing out over the three central sections. This gave him a figure something like a sixpointed star (Figure 17a). He then went on to divide each of the twelve sides of this star into three equal parts, again constructing equilateral triangles. This gave the even more prickly curve drawn in Figure 17b. After infinitely many divisions and constructions of right triangles he obtained a curve at each point of which there was a break or a prickle.

Mathematicians constructed many continuous functions whose graphs possess a tangent at no point, and began to study their properties. These

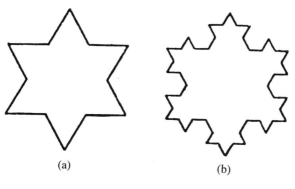

(a)   (b)

Figure 17

properties have no similarity to those of the "well-behaved" smooth functions with which they had dealt up to that time. It is no wonder, then, that mathematicians trained in the classical tradition regarded these new functions with astonishment. Going even beyond this, the prominent exponent of classical analysis Charles Hermite[14] wrote as follows to his friend, the Dutch mathematician Stieltjes[15]: "I turn away in horror from this regrettable plague of continuous functions that do not have a derivative at even one point" (i.e., as we have named them, everywhere-prickly curves).

In physics we encounter curves highly reminiscent of the everywhere prickly curves of von Koch and others. These curves are the trajectories of particles undergoing Brownian motion caused by collisions with molecules. The French scientist J. Perrin[16] made a sketch of the motion of these particles. He observed their positions every 30 seconds and connected the points thus obtained with straight line segments. His result was a tangle of broken lines something like that sketched in Figure 18. But it should not be thought that the particles observed actually moved in straight lines between the separate observations. If Perrin had observed them every half second instead of every half minute, he would have had to replace each straight line segment by a much more complicated broken line like that in Figure 18. And the shorter the interval between observations, the more complicated and "prickly" the broken line would become. The American mathematician N. Wiener[17] showed that if the particles in Brownian motion are sufficiently small that their inertia can be neglected, they move along curves which have no tangent at any point.

A closed curve of infinite length. We have often encountered curves of infinite length: the straight line, the parabola, etc., all have infinite length. But all these

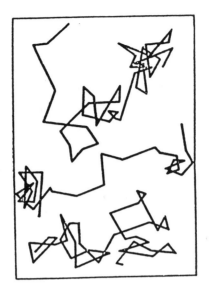

Figure 18

curves go off to infinity, so it is not surprising that they have infinite length. However, it is not difficult to construct a curve entirely contained in a finite region of the plane and still having infinite length. For this we can take a circle and wind a spiral with infinitely many turns around it. Since the number of turns is infinite and the length of each turn is greater that that of the circumference of the circle, the length of the spiral must be infinite.

But can we construct a closed curve of infinite length? The ordinary closed curves - the circle, the ellipse, the cardioid - all have finite length. However, the length of von Koch's prickly curve is infinite. Indeed, the perimeter of the original triangle is 3. As is easily computed, the star obtained in the first stage has length 4. And in the following stage we obtain a curve composed of 48 segments each of length 1/9. Thus its perimeter is 48/9. Next we obtain a curve of length 192/27, etc. In general, at the nth stage we obtain a curve with perimeter $3 \cdot (\frac{4}{3})^n$. But this expression approaches infinity as n increases, so that the length of von Koch's curve is infinite.

A mathematical carpet. It is told that Catherine the Second asked one of her generals what the difference is between a mortar and a howitzer. The embarrassed general replied: "You see, Queen Mother, a mortar is one thing and a howitzer is something else." We would probably receive an informative

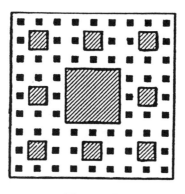

Figure 19

answer like this one if we were to ask a person knowing little about mathematics what the difference is between a curve, a surface and a solid. Moreover, he would be surprised that we asked about such obvious things. After all, it is quite clear that a curve, a surface, and a solid are quite different things, and no one would call a circle a surface or a sphere a curve.

But a witty chess master once said that the difference between a master and a beginning chess player is that the beginner has everything clearly fixed in his mind, while to the master everything is a mystery. That is also how matters stand with our question. Of course, when we are speaking of such geometric figures as a circle or the perimeter of a square, no one has any doubts that these are curves and not surfaces. But in the course of mathematical development, since Cantor's discoveries, there have appeared many strange geometric figures, and even an experienced, knowledgeable professor, not to speak of a student, will not be able to decide right away whether they are curves, surfaces, or solids.

We shall present some of these figures.

We take a square of side 1 and divide it into 9 equal parts; then we discard the central part (leaving the sides of the discarded square). After this we divide each of the remaining squares into 9 equal squares, and again discard the central squares. After one more such operation we arrive at the figure drawn in Figure 19 (the squares to be discarded are hatched). It is clear that the figure in Figure 19 is still a surface. But we will not stop at the third step; the squares will be divided into nine equal parts infinitely many times, and each time the central part will be discarded. In the end we obtain a geometric figure called *Sierpiński's carpet* after the Polish mathematician who devised it.

The figure looks like cloth woven by some mad weaver. The threads of

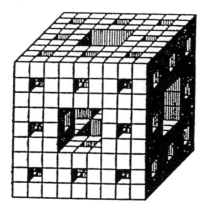

Figure 20

warp and woof run down and across and interlace to form a very symmetric and beautiful design. But the resulting carpet is full of holes – there is not an uncut piece in it; even the smallest square had to have its center cut out.

And it is not at all clear whether this carpet is a curve or a surface. After all, on the one hand, it does not contain a single whole piece, and so can hardly be called a surface; but, on the other hand, the threads forming it were woven into such a complex pattern that probably no one would unhesitatingly call Sierpiński's carpet a curve. In any case, it would be very hard to draw this "curve."

But Sierpiński's carpet is not the most complicated geometric figure. Instead of a square we could have taken a cube, divided it into 27 equal small cubes and discarded the central small cube along with its 6 neighboring cubes. Then we would have divided each small remaining cube into 27 equal parts and again would have carried out the operation of discarding certain parts (the solid remaining after two such operations is shown in Figure 20). Suppose that the operation had been carried out infinitely many times. What kind of figure would we get after all the pieces had been discarded – a curve, a surface or a solid?

Euclid does not rely on Euclid. When a complicated geometric problem was placed before mathematicians of an earlier time, they first proceeded to examine what Euclid had written about it. After all, for almost two thousand years Euclid was the standard of mathematical rigor and an encyclopedia of geometric knowledge. It is significant that even philosophers, striving to secure themselves from reproach regarding the rigor of their arguments, had recourse to Euclid's language and formulated their statements as axioms, lemmas, and theorems.

But as far as our question is concerned, everything Euclid wrote was entirely too vague. The first lines of Euclid's book *Elements* read as follows:

1. A point is that which has no parts.

2. A curve is length without width.

3. The extremity of a curve is a point.

4. A surface is that which has only length and width.

5. The extremity of a surface is a curve.

6. A boundary is that which is the extremity of something.

7. A figure is that which is contained within something or within some boundaries.

Now, like these or not, they are not rigorous mathematical definitions. A person not knowing what points, curves, or lines are will hardly get much useful information from these "definitions," so reminiscent of the answer of the confused general ("a curve is one thing, and a surface is something else"). And, in any case, we shall not succeed in finding out from these definitions whether Sierpiński's carpet is a curve or a surface, whether it has just length without width or both length and width.

However, such complicated figures as Sierpiński's carpet were unknown in Euclid's time, and definitions were not really necessary for simple figures – everyone could pick out which were the curves and which were the surfaces in a figure. It seems though, that Euclid himself felt that not all was right with his definitions of the fundamental concepts. In any case, having presented these definitions at the beginning of the book, he went on to completely forget about them and did not employ them even once in the remainder of his work.

Are rigorous definitions needed? Euclid's authority stood unquestioned for two thousand years. To doubt his statements in any way was to decisively and irrevocably undermine your own mathematical reputation. One of the greatest mathematicians of the 19th century, Carl Friedrich Gauss, arrived at the idea of a non-Euclidean geometry even before Lobachevski, but did not publish his investigations, fearing, as he wrote one friend, the screams of the Boeotians.[*]

It was finally the mathematical exploit of the great Russian geometer Nikolai Ivanovich Lobachevski, who did publish his discoveries in spite of the derision of the uncomprehending savants, that gave the world non-Euclidean geometry.

It became clear after the appearance of Lobachevski's work that there exist two geometries, both irreproachable logically, but arriving at entirely different theorems. But if this is so, then every appeal to "geometric obviousness" completely lost its value. Each geometric assertion now had to be based on rigorous definitions and irreproachable logical arguments. And now it was especially important that the fundamental geometric concepts of curve, figure, and solid be given exact definitions, in no way like those of the type "this is one thing, and that is something else."

This attempt at rigorous definition characterized not only the geometry, but also the analysis of the 19th century.

Science had succeeded in solving the most varied problems, from calculating the trajectory of an artillery shell to predicting the motions of planets and comets, with the aid of the differential and integral calculus based on the work of Newton, Leibniz, Euler, Lagrange,[18] and other great mathematicians of the 17th and 18th centuries. But the fundamental concepts with whose aid these remarkable results were achieved were defined in a highly unrigorous manner. The mathematical analysis of that time was based on the concept of an infinitesimal quantity, something balancing on the border of existence and nonexistence; something like zero, but not really zero. And mathematicians of the 18th century were forced to encourage their dubious students with the words: "Work, and belief will come to you."

But, mathematics is not religion; it cannot be founded on faith. And what was most important, the methods yielding such remarkable results in the hands of the great masters began to lead to errors and paradoxes when employed by their less talented students. The masters were kept from error by their perfect mathematical intuition, that subconscious feeling that often leads to the right answer more quickly than lengthy logical reasoning. But the students did not possess this intuition, and the end of the 18th century was marked by an unprecedented scandal in mathematics – an influx of formulas worth less than the paper they were printed on and questionable theorems whose domain of applicability was entirely unclear.

So, like children who break a beautiful toy in order to see what makes it work, 19th-century mathematicians subjected all the concepts employed up to that time to a severe critique and then began to rebuild mathematics on a

---

[*] A proverbially dull Greek tribe.

foundation of rigorous definitions. Appeals to intuition were rejected; in place of this they demanded the most rigorous logic. [*] Found wanting in logic were the simple statements met with in a course in analysis, such as: "Consider the domain *G* bounded by the closed curve Γ." What is a closed curve? Why is it the boundary of a domain? Into how many parts does a closed curve divide the plane, and which of the these parts is being studied?

The mathematicians of the 18th century did not reply to these questions. They just drew an oval and thought that this was all that needed to be done. But no one believed in pictures in the 19th century. The question "what is a curve?" was only one of the vital questions facing analysts.

However, a long time went by before they succeeded in giving a comprehensive answer to this question.

A curve is the path of a moving point. In order to arrive at a rigorous definition of curve it was necessary to move away from the concrete objects on which the formation of the mathematical concept was based: long, thin threads; light rays; long, narrows roads, etc. In all these cases the length is so much greater than the width that the latter can be neglected. After mathematical idealization we arrive at the notion of length without width.

The first to try to give a rigorous definition of curve was the French mathematician Camille Jordan.[19] He proceeded from the fact that the trajectory of the motion of a very small body may be represented by a long, narrow tube. As we diminish the size of the body, the tube becomes more and more narrow and in the limit becomes the trajectory of a moving point – a curve possessing no width. Jordan applied this image in his definition of curve. Namely, he called the trajectory of a moving point a curve. Here the point is to move in a continuous manner, not making any jumps.

Jordan's definition can be more exactly stated as follows: In order to determine the position of a moving point its coordinates must be given for each moment during the motion. Since the motion takes place over a finite time interval, we can assume without loss of generality that this interval is [0,1]. In other words, the point begins to move at some moment of time taken as the start of the observation and completes its motion after a certain unit of time has elapsed (a second, a minute, a year, etc.). The coordinates of the moving point are given for each moment of time *t* during the passing of this interval. Thus, the coordinates of the point depend on the moment of time *t*, and so are

---

[*]True, they frequently tended to throw out the baby with the bathwater; in the 20th century much of what was thrown out became once more part of science.

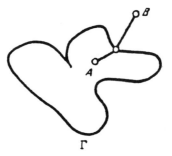

Figure 21

functions of t. We shall denote these functions by $f(t)$ and $g(t)$:

$$x = f(t) \quad y = g(t)$$

The requirement that the point move continuously amounts to the requirement that the functions $f(t)$ and $g(t)$ be continuous at each point of the segment [0,1]. Roughly speaking, a small change in t should produce only a small change in the functions $f(t)$ and $g(t)$.

Jordan's definition turned out to be a rather successful one. All the curves with which mathematicians had dealt up to this time turned out to be curves in Jordan's sense, or, as we say, *Jordan curves*. Curves made up of arcs of different curves are also Jordan curves.

The theorem is obvious, but the proof is not. Employing his concept of curve, Jordan was successful in giving a precise meaning to the sentence from the analysis textbook that we spoke of earlier: "Let the closed curve Γ bound the domain G." A closed Jordan curve is a curve which at $t = 1$ passes through the point that was passed through at $t = 0$. The curve does not intersect itself as long as no two values of time t_1 and t_2 between 0 and 1 correspond to the same point on the curve.

Jordan proved the following theorem.

A closed Jordan curve Γ which does not intersect itself divides the plane into two parts. Two points contained in the same part can be connected by a broken line that does not intersect the curve Γ, but two points contained in different parts cannot be connected by such a broken line; any broken line connecting them must intersect the curve Γ (Figure 21).

This theorem seems completely obvious. Its proof, however, required very subtle arguments. Even when the curve Γ is the boundary of a polygon, the proof remains quite complicated.

The two parts into which a closed Jordan curve divides the plane are called the exterior and interior domains bounded by this curve. The concept of a domain bounded by a closed curve thus acquired an exact meaning.

A curve passing through all the points of a square. It appeared at first when Jordan gave his definition of a curve that the goal had been achieved; a rigorous definition of the concept of a curve was now available that did not depend on intuition. But it was quickly found out that this was not the case – Jordan's definition embraced not only what mathematicians usually called curves, but also geometric figures that no one would call curves. Mathematicians could somehow reconcile themselves to everywhere-prickly curves, but no one had the heart to call a square a curve. But it did turn out that the square, the triangle (not the perimeter of the figure, but in each case the figure itself with all its interior points) and the disk were curves in Jordan's sense. This was proved by the Italian mathematician Peano.[20]

We already mentioned that Cantor set up a one-to-one correspondence between the points of a segment and those of a square, i.e., he showed that there are just as many points on the segment as are in the square (see p.65). But his correspondence was not continuous. As the point moved along the segment, the corresponding point on the square did not crawl around like a beetle, but jumped around like a flea. Indeed, let us take the points

$$0.50000000\ldots \quad \text{and} \quad 0.499999990000000\ldots$$

on the segment. These points are quite close together. But the corresponding points on the square are far apart. For the point corresponding to the first of these is $(0.50000\ldots, 0.0000\ldots)$ situated on the bottom of the square, while the point corresponding to the second is $(0.4999000\ldots, 0.9999000\ldots)$ situated very close to the top of the square. And if we increase the number of nines in the second point, thus bringing it closer to the first, the corresponding points on the square do not begin to approach one another.

Thus, Cantor's mapping of the segment onto the square, although one-to-one, was not continuous, and so did not give rise to a Jordan curve. Peano succeeded in setting up another mapping of the set of points of the segment onto the set of points of the square which sent neighboring points on the segment into neighboring points on the square. In other words, Peano was able to construct a curve (in Jordan's sense) which passed through all the points of the square.

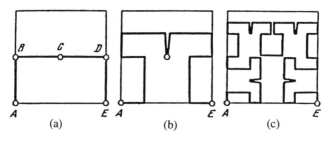

Figure 22

But, after all, the square is uniform, so we will not be able to see where the curve begins, where it ends and how it moves about the square. Therefore, we shall follow the example of the physicist Perrin, rather than that of an abstract painter, and sketch the position of the moving point using line segments. The shorter the intervals of time taken between separate "observations," the more accurately will the broken line thus obtained represent Peano's curve.

We shall first observe the position of the moving point every $\frac{1}{4}$ second. In other words, we observe its position at the beginning of the motion, at $\frac{1}{4}$ second after the beginning of the motion, at $\frac{1}{2}$ second after the beginning of the motion, at $\frac{3}{4}$ second, and at the end of the motion. This gives us 5 points. Connecting them, we obtain the line *ABCDE* drawn in Figure 22a.

Naturally, this line does not pass through all points of the square. Now we reduce the interval of time between individual observations and observe the position of the point every $\frac{1}{16}$ second. Now the curve twists more, the number of breaks increases, and it takes the form sketched in Figure 22b. If we observe the position of the moving point still more often, we obtain the curve sketched in Figure 22c. We see that the curve fills the square more and more densely, that it approaches more and more closely to each of its points. In the limit, in which we would be constantly observing the moving point, we would obtain a curve passing through all points of the square without exception.

It should be noted that, while Peano has an advantage over Cantor in that his curve is continuous, he falls short in another respect. His curve no longer gives rise to a one-to-one mapping of the segment onto the the square; it passes through some points of the square several times. It was later proved that it is impossible to obtain a correspondence that is *both* one-to-one *and* continuous: there does not exist a Jordan curve passing through all the points of the square exactly once!

Everything had come unstrung. It is difficult to put into words the effect that Peano's result had on the mathematical world. It seemed that everything was in ruins, that all the basic mathematical concepts had lost their meaning; the difference between curve and surface, between surface and solid was no longer clear. (The result showing the impossibility of a one-to-one continuous correspondence between the segment and the square was still unknown.) Poincaré bitterly exclaimed: "How is it possible that intuition could so deceive us?"

It soon became clear that Jordan's definition had its faults. On the one hand it was too broad: Peano's curve fits it. But on the other hand it was too narrow. For example, a circle with a spiral wrapped around it is not a Jordan curve.

So the question was again raised: what is a curve and how does it differ from a surface? The answer is related to Cantor's general studies of geometric figures.

How to make a statue. Having founded the theory of sets, Cantor now turned his attention to the question: *what is a geometric figure?* The most general answer to this question would read: a geometric figure is any set of points in space. If this set lies in the plane, then we obtain a plane geometric figure. But this answer would be too general – a "figure" in this sense would have no really interesting properties. The geometry of such figures would be almost devoid of theorems.

So it was first of all necessary to limit the class of sets to be studied, separating out those which had properties close to those of ordinary geometric figures.

In order to separate out this class of figures we have to decide what it is that ordinary figures such as the square, disk, line segment, etc., have in common. It turns out that we can construct all these figures by means of a single procedure.

When Rodin was asked how he managed to make his remarkable statues, he replied: "I choose a block of marble and chop off whatever I don't need."

We can obtain any "reasonable" bounded plane geometric figure by this same method: we take a square which contains it and chop off whatever we do not need. Of course, we do not chop everything off at once, but proceed step by step, at each step removing disks. Here we remove the interior of the disk while its boundary, a circle, is left in the figure. Briefly, we are removing an *open disk.*

At first we might think that this procedure would only yield figures like those in Figure 23. But the secret lies in the fact that we remove not just one or two disks, but a countable set of disks. In this way we can obtain any "reasonable" figure we like. To see this, note that the set of disks with rational radii and

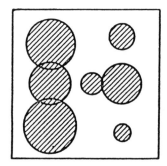

Figure 23

centers is countable. (This is easily shown by the methods of Chapter 2.) To obtain a required figure we need only remove from a square that contains it (the "block of marble") all open rational disks that don't contain a single one of its points. And if we remove such disks from the plane rather than from a square, then we can obtain unbounded figures as well.

Using the procedure just described we can obtain disks and squares, ellipses and astroids, regular polygons and stars, but *not* a square minus a single vertex. This is because removing the vertex would entail removing a neighborhood of that vertex. Figures obtained from the plane by removing from it a countable number of open disks are said to be *closed*.

Continua. In addition to the ordinary geometric figures, it turns out that by removing a countable set of open disks (or squares, etc.) we can also obtain other sets quite unlike the ordinary figures but still possessing many interesting properties. For instance, Sierpiński's carpet, of which we have already spoken at length, can be obtained in the following manner: from the square of side 1 discard small squares one by one, leaving their sides behind.

However, this discarding process can yield "figures" not composed of a single whole piece. For example, if we remove "crosses,"[*] as in Figure 24, in the end we obtain a set not containing a single whole piece. (Such a set is said to be *completely disconnected*). Hence, we make the requirement that after each discarding operation there must remain a set consisting of a single piece. Then after all the removals there will remain a set composed of a single piece (or, as mathematicians say, a *connected set*). The set obtained will also

---

[*]Including terminal segments such as, for example, the segments AB, CD, EF, GH.

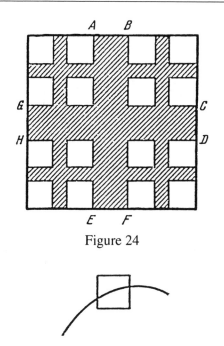

Figure 24

Figure 25

be bounded, i.e., it is entirely contained in some square.

A set F satisfying the following conditions:

1. it is obtained from a square by discarding a countable set of open disks (or squares, etc.),

2. it is composed of a single piece (it is connected),

was said by Cantor to be a *continuum* (recall that the Latin word *continuum* means unbroken). A continuum turns out to be the most general set still possessing properties quite similar to those of ordinary geometric figures.

Cantor curves. Now we are in a position to answer the question: what is a plane curve? Since plane curves must be geometric figures, it is clear that we must search for them among the continua. But a square and disk are continua, and we certainly do not want to call these figures curves. Thus, we have to add on some other requirement which would eliminate such figures.

Note that both the circle and the square contain whole pieces of the plane. But a curve would not contain whole pieces of the plane; no matter how small

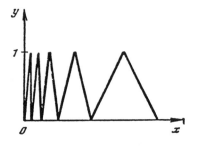

Figure 26

a square we took, there would always be points on it not belonging to the curve
(Figure 25).

So here is the supplementary condition we need:

*A plane curve in Cantor's sense is a continuum contained in the plane which
does not fill a whole piece of the plane* (i.e., in every square there are points not
belonging to this curve).

For example, a segment, the perimeter of a triangle, a circle, and a four-leaf
rose are curves. So is the Sierpiński carpet; indeed, we put a hole in *every*
square obtained in the division process involved in its construction, so that no
whole piece of the plane is contained in it. Other Cantor curves include a circle
with a spiral wound around it and the saw-toothed curve of Figure 26 together
with the segment [0,1] of the y-axis. More generally, all those figures that seem
to our intuition to be curves are also curves in Cantor's sense, while any figure
containing even one whole piece of the plane does not belong to the class of
Cantor curves.

But even among Cantor curves are some whose properties are quite unlike
those of ordinary curves. We shall now discuss some of these.

Can a curve have area? Of course, now that the reader has made the acquaintance of curves passing through all the points of a square, he will not be
surprised by anything. But even so, can a curve have area? After all, Euclid
did say that a curve is length without width. And how can we get area from
something without width? Cantor's definition of a curve, too, says that the
curve cannot contain a whole piece of the plane. Where will we find area in
this case? But we have seen many times that infinite processes lead to entirely
unexpected results.

Before we study the question, we must come to an understanding about
the exact meaning of the words used. What is meant by the words "*a curve*

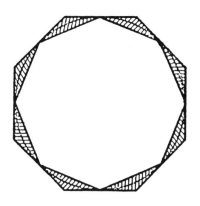

Figure 27

has zero area" or "*a curve has nonzero area*"? Let us take the most ordinary curve– a straight line segment. Since its width is zero, we can place it inside a rectangle of arbitrarily small area; we only have to choose a rectangle of sufficiently small width. In exactly the same way we can put a circle inside a polygonal domain of arbitrarily small area. This can be done by inscribing in it a regular polygon with a very large number of sides and then circumscribing a similar polygon. The region included between the two polygons will have small area (the more sides our polygons have, the smaller the area), and the circle is entirely contained in this region (Figure 27).

Now it is clear what is meant by the words *a curve has zero area*. They mean that no matter how small a positive number ε we take, we can find a polygonal domain which contains the curve and has an area less than ε. And if we cannot find such a domain, the area of the curve is not equal to zero.

In order to make the definition clearer we shall apply it to a more complicated curve than a simple segment or circle. Sierpiński's carpet represents, of course, a very complicated curve. Let us find its area. Recall first that the area of the whole square was 1. In the first step we discarded the central square of area 1/9. We thus got a polygonal domain of area 8/9. In the second step we discarded 8 squares each of which has area 1/81. This left a polygonal domain of area

$$\frac{8}{9} - \frac{8}{81} = \frac{64}{81} = (\frac{8}{9})^2 \ .$$

It is now clear that after the third step there will remain a polygonal domain of area $(8/9)^3$, after the fourth a domain with area $(8/9)^4$, etc. But if you

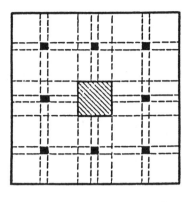

Figure 28

take any proper fraction and raise it to higher and higher powers, the result tends to zero. This tells us that for every $\varepsilon > 0$, after sufficiently many steps, we get a polygonal domain of area less than ε. And this domain covers Sierpiński's carpet. Hence the area of Sierpiński's carpet is zero.

This would seem to mark the complete triumph of Euclid's definition. Even such a complicated curve as Sierpiński's carpet has area zero. But it would be premature to celebrate the triumph now. After all, no one forced us to discard such large pieces. Figure 28 illustrates a more economical way of removing squares. If we choose squares of the right size, then the total area of the removed squares won't exceed $\frac{1}{2}$. But then after each step of the removal process we are left with a polygonal domain of area not less than $\frac{1}{2}$. The figure left over after completion of our process cannot be covered by a polygonal domain of area less than $\frac{1}{2}$. Therefore its area cannot be said to be zero. Now, this remainder, just as in the case of Sierpiński's carpet, is a curve (in Cantor's sense) – in constructing it we made a hole in every square and rectangle and not a single whole rectangle or square was left behind.

As a result, therefore, a curve in Cantor's sense can have nonzero area!

Domains without area. The example we just analyzed is not too convincing: the curve we obtained consists of points of self-intersection and does not bound any domain. So the question arises: can a "good" curve that does not intersect itself have nonzero area? It happens that it can!

We can construct such a curve by changing a little the construction carried out before. We first construct a set in which you not only cannot find a whole piece of square, but not even a whole piece of curve, and the area of this set

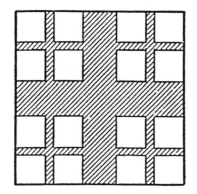

Figure 29

will not be zero. To do this we must discard whole crosses rather than central squares, as shown in Figure 29. Here we select the dimensions of the discarded figures so that their combined area is less than half the area of the whole square. But then the area of the leftover set is at least half the area of the whole square. Note that in constructing the set we discarded whole crosses, ruthlessly tearing up the square. No two points of the set remaining can be connected by a curve, not even a curve in Cantor's sense; every connection between its points has been broken. As mathematicians would say, the remainder is a completely disconnected set. And still the area of this set, not containing a single whole piece of the plane nor an arc of a curve, is different from zero; you cannot cover this set with a polygonal domain of area less than 1/2.

Now it is easy to construct an example of a closed curve that does not intersect itself and has nonzero area. To do this we need only connect the points we already have, just as we drew a curve through all the points of the square. And because we discarded whole crosses at each step, our curve will not intersect itself (in this it differs from Peano's curve). But since it passes through all points of the set, whose area must be at least 1/2, the area of the curve obtained must be at least 1/2.

It is also no trouble now to construct a domain without area. For this we need only connect two points A and B of our curve with some kind of curve, perhaps a semicircle. Then we obtain a curve which bounds some domain G. And what is its area? The answer depends on whether or not we include the boundary with the domain – after all, the boundary itself has an area of at least 1/2. Clearly, our domain has no area in the ordinary sense of the word. In mathematics domains with no area in the usual sense are called *nonsquareable*.

And yet, they can be measured. Mathematicians had thought about what is meant by the area of a figure before the discovery of nonsquarable figures. Before that, scholars used the notions of length, area, and volume without subjecting them to rigorous critical analysis. The story is told of a French "circle squarer" who brought his "solution" to the Paris Academy of Science. Asked what he meant by the area of a circle the man exclaimed: "You don't define areas, you compute them." And this very point of view was also widespread among mathematicians. They thought that area is a number associated with a geometric figure and having obvious properties (the area of a figure is the sum of the areas of its parts, congruent figures have the same area, and so on). Not for a moment did they doubt that every plane figure has area (possibly equal to zero or infinite).

A characteristic of mathematics is that it pursues new methods of solution of practical problems, studies and sharpens its tools, and looks for the widest and most natural area of applicability for each new concept and for the most general conditions of validity of each proved theorem. All this is a necessity and not the frivolous pastime of mathematical snobs. Only by establishing concepts and theorems in greatest generality and by freeing them from unnecessary restrictions related to the concrete problems from which they arose can one see the connections between distant areas of science and learn to use methods created in one context in situations which, at first sight, have nothing in common with that context.

That is why such seemingly obvious concepts as length, area and volume (later to be subsumed under the single concept of measure) were subjected to detailed analysis. One of the first mathematicians who tried to make precise the concept of measure was Jordan. For many decades he presented in Paris a course of mathematical analysis based on precise definitions, flawless proofs, and rigorous logic. Of course, he couldn't use in his lectures the vague concept of area. His definition of area can be stated as follows: the area of a figure is a number between the areas of polygons contained in that figure and the areas of polygons containing that figure. It turned out that the only figures that have Jordan area are figures whose boundary has zero area. Unfortunately, very many figures have no Jordan area. In particular, the nonsquarable figures described earlier have no Jordan area.

Inspired by Jordan's lectures, young scholars tackled the problem. At the end of the 19th century, Emile Borel[21] proposed one of the first definitions applicable to a very wide class of figures. He observed that all figures used in science, regardless of whether they are on a line, in the plane, or in space, can be obtained from very simple figures – segmen.'s, squares, and cubes – by means of the two operations of forming countable ι nions of sets and taking complements of sets (in particular, as we saw earlier, all closed sets can be obtained in this way). By transfinite alternation of these operations one can obtain even more complex sets, called *B*-sets in Borel's honor. (Using Zeno's idea, we can obtain all such sets in a finite time interval by constantly doubling the speed of the operations involved.)

It turned out that one can assign to each Borel set a number as its measure by relying on the following two principles:

1. *If a set A is representable as a countable union of disjoint measurable subsets then its measure is the sum of the measures of these subsets;*

2. *The measure of the complement of a measurable subset is the difference between the measure of the whole and the measure of that subset.*

In particular, Borel's principles imply that the measure of a countable set is zero (such a set consists of countably many points each of which has measure zero).

Unfortunately, it later turned out that Borel's process has a serious short-coming. It is obvious that the measure of a set must not depend on the way in which it is built up from simple sets. And Borel was unable to produce the required proof of this independence.

Henri Lebesgue,[22] who began his scientific work at that time, proceeded differently. Before we discuss his approach to the measure problem we say something about his earlier achievements.

Lebesgue's first papers angered classical mathematicians. The very title of one of them, "On unruled developable surfaces," seemed to them as outlandish as, say "On gaseous ice" to a physicist or "On fishlike elephants" to a biologist. Even bad students knew that a developable surface (a cylinder, a cone, and so on) is made up of straight lines, that it can be obtained by the motion of a rectilinear generator. But the source of the trouble was that the young author thought of developable surfaces in a way different from that of the classical geometers. He regarded as developable not only surfaces obtained by carefully bending a sheet of paper but also surfaces obtained by crumpling it (in explaining his paper to a friend Lebesgue said: "Imagine a crumpled handkerchief"). He showed that one can so "crumple" a piece of paper that it doesn't contain a single straight-line segment. Of course, the resulting surface is all folds and breaks, which is why it was missed by geometers who classified developable surfaces. They studied only the smooth case.

Next Lebesgue tackled the problem of the area of a non-smooth surface, a surface that admits no tangent planes anywhere. For a crumpled developable surface the problem has a simple solution: one flattens it and computes the area of the resulting piece of the plane. But this answer can not be obtained from the formulas of classical mathematics. The latter apply only to smooth surfaces.

An attempt to measure the area of a surface by approximating it by the areas of inscribed polyhedra is bound to fail. In fact, the German mathematician Hermann Schwarz[23] showed that this approach fails even in the case of an ordinary cylinder. Specifically, Schwarz showed that one can inscribe in a cylinder a polyhedron with so many folds that its area is far greater than that of the cylinder. Lebesgue managed to come up with a definition of the area of a surface that dispensed with the need for tangent planes and avoided the difficulties connected with the "Schwarz accordion." Work on this special problem brought Lebesgue to general ideas of the measure of sets and enabled him to find a way of measuring the lengths, areas, and volumes of the strangest figures.

Lebesgue took from Borel the idea of summing series and modified Jordan's definition of measure by using, in addition to polygons, figures obtained by forming countable unions of polygons. Specifically, a figure is *Lebesgue* ε-*coverable* if it can be covered by a countable union of polygons such that the sum of the series of their areas is less than ε. Now call a set X *Lebesgue-measurable* if for every $\varepsilon > 0$ it can be represented as a polygon A_ε to which one adds an ε-coverable set and from which one removes another ε-coverable set. If $|A|$ denotes the measure of a polygon A, then, clearly, the measure of the set X must lie between the numbers $|A_\varepsilon| - \varepsilon$ and $|A_\varepsilon| + \varepsilon$. If turns out that for Lebesgue-measurable sets there always exists just one number with this property regardless of the choice of $\varepsilon > 0$ and of the approximating polygon A_ε. This number is called the *Lebesgue measure of the set* X.

The concept of Lebesgue measure turned out to be an unqualified success. It was found to apply to all sets encountered in science up to that time. Subsequently discovered instances of nonmeasurable sets involved the use of the *axiom of choice* (to be discussed below) and were not constructive. We can therefore say that Lebesgue solved the problem of measure for all sets encountered in mathematical practice.

By means of his concept of measure Lebesgue could obtain the integrals of all discontinuous functions that could be constructed by the methods of that time. Predictably, the integral based on Lebesgue measure is called the *Lebesgue integral*.

The triumph of Lebesgues' ideas brought Gaston Darboux[24] to a change of heart. Darboux had been one of the leaders of the classical mathematicians. But at the international mathematical congress that took place in Rome in 1909 Darboux spoke of the fervent and inquisitive spirit of 20th century mathematics, about science that pursued its investigations in a completely new area with unexplored perspectives. He stressed that 20th century science does not hesitate to probe the very foundations of the constructions that had seemed unshakeable for so long.

Later, the ideas that resulted in the creation of Lebesgue measure and the Lebesgue integral enabled Kolmogorov to construct an axiomatic theory of probability and Norbert Wiener to define the concepts of measure and integral for spaces of functions. All who worked with the ideas of measure relied on constructions and theorems that originated with Lebesgue. After the publication of the works of Kolmogorov just referred to, these ideas began to be widely used in the theory of probability and its applications, and, in particular, in statistical physics. They were also applied in the study of dynamical systems. As for theoretical mathematics, the importance of the Lebesgue integral cannot be overestimated. Suffice it to say that many of its most important results could not even be formulated without the Lebesgue integral. It was not for nothing that the hymn of "Luzitania," a group of young Soviet mathematicians who in the 20s studied the newest results in the theory of functions, proclaimed that "Our god is Lebesgue, Our idol the integral." The group "Luzitania," a name that honors N.N. Luzin, founder of the Russian school of functions of a real variable and teacher of the members of that group, merits more than a mere reference. Indeed, it is difficult to overestimate its importance in the study of mathematical problems involving infinite sets.

Luzitania. The developments just described resulted in a new theory of functions. Interest in this theory grew in an extraordinary manner. In Göttingen, Hilbert and his school used the concept of the Lebesgue integral to study the circle of problems involving so-called integral equations, and Italian mathematicians proved a number of extremely interesting results.

In the 19th century, St. Petersburg was the acknowledged center of Russian science. Within the walls of the St. Petersburg Academy of Science, the traditions of Euler and Daniel Bernoulli were piously preserved. Here labored great Russian mathematicians – Ostrogradski,[25] Chebyshev,[26] A.A. Markov,[27] Lyapunov,[28] Steklov,[29] and Korkin.[30] They all had in common an intense interest in investigations dealing with mathematical analysis and in the solution of difficult, concrete mathematical problems. The newfangled investigations in set theory and in the theory of discontinuous functions did not appeal to them. These investigations struck them as far removed from the problems they were studying (although it turned out later that results obtained by following these newfangled roads were of great use in many traditional areas of mathematics).

Things were different in the old Russian capital. Here, at the famous Moscow university, courses in set theory were offered as early as the beginning of the 20th century and in 1907 I.I. Zhegalkin[31] defended a master's thesis on transfinite numbers. One of the people who got interested in this realm of ideas was the differential geometer D.F. Egorov,[32] one of the best Moscow mathematicians of that time. He was able to prove a theorem about the convergence of series that became one of the most important tools in all studies in the theory of functions. What was most important, however, was that Egorov drew the attention of his young students to this area of research. One of these students, who was just embarking on a scientific career, was Luzin.

At that time many scholars tried to understand the relation between the "wild" functions of Dirichlet, Riemann, Borel and Lebesgue and the functions studied by the previous generations of scholars. Luzin found that by "adjusting" a discontinuous function on a set of arbitrarily small measure one can turn it into a continuous function. And a continuous function can be approximated with arbitrary closeness by a polynomial. Thus the most tangled functions can, in a sense, be reduced to the best known functions, namely polynomials.

Luzin also studied problems connected with trigonometric (Fourier) series, an issue of abiding interest to specialists in the theory of functions of a real variable since the time of Cantor's earliest papers. In this area too Luzin proved a number of extremely interesting results that disclosed some of the subtle mechanisms that control the convergence of these series. These, and many other results he had proved, were the basis of his master's dissertation titled "Integrals and trigonometric series." The scientific merit of his thesis was so great that, notwithstanding the opposition of some mathematicians of the classical persuasion, he was awarded for it a doctorate in pure mathematics – a very rare event in the practice of Russian universities.

Luzin's scientific enthusiasm, the novelty of his ideas, and his outstanding teaching abilities attracted to him the most talented young mathematicians, most of whom had been associated with him since their school days. Many of them obtained outstanding scientific results even before the completion of their university studies. For many years mathematicians had tried to show that if a Fourier series converges to zero almost everywhere (that is, everywhere except for a set of measure zero) then its coefficients must all be equal to zero. To everybody's amazement the student D.E. Men'shov[33] showed that this is not the case. His counterexample, like many brilliant ones constructed by Luzin himself, was very intricate. Men'shov's paper was the first in a series of investigations devoted to the class of problems he discovered. N.K. Bari,[34] who later wrote a splendid book on Fourier series, obtained strong results in this area. In his student days Kolmogorov also worked on a number of problems in the theory of Fourier series. He constructed a remarkable example of a Lebesgue-integrable function whose Fourier series diverges everywhere.

In another direction, Luzin's students worked on the structure of Borel sets. To show that a Borel set is either countable or contains a subset of the cardinality of the continuum, Pavel Sergeevich Aleksandrov, while still a student, invented an extremely subtle construction (called in his honor the *A*-operation) that can be used to obtain any such set. Some time later, M.Ya. Suslin,[35] another young student of Luzin's, showed that the *A*-operation can be used to obtain certain sets that are not Borel sets. This gave rise to the problem of describing this class of sets now known as Suslin sets. Unhappily, Suslin's premature death from typhus in 1919 put an end to his research. It was continued by Luzin, who was joined by P.S. Novikov[36] and Liudmila Keldysh.[37] Their results gave rise to a new branch of mathematics known as *descriptive set theory*. Further work in this area touched on the very core of the foundations of set theory and showed the bounds of set-theoretic thought. Many problems that are now solved were posed by Luzin and the results obtained confirm his remarkable intuition.

The work of Luzin and his students made Moscow the universally acknowledged center of research in the area of functions of a real variable. This state of affairs was not affected by either World War I, or the civil war, or the intervention, or the blockade. In Poland, Luzin's ideas were developed by W. Sierpiński,[38] who lived in Moscow during W.W.I and associated with Luzin.

We have mentioned only some of Luzin's many students. Many of them have achieved international fame.

Due to their intense preoccupation with problems of set theory and the theory of functions of a real variable, members of the Luzitania group tended at times to underestimate the importance of classical directions in mathematics. But the scientific interests of many of them shifted later to areas much closer to practical problems. For example, as mentioned earlier, Kolmogorov used the ideas of Lebesgue measure in the theory of probability and then studied its practical applications. Similarly, the outstanding applied mathematician M.A.

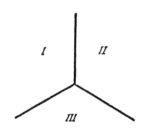

Figure 30

Lavrent'ev[39] studied the subtlest issues of set theory in his youth.

The great irrigation project. It would take a book on the history of Soviet mathematics to describe the areas of mathematics pursued by former members of the Luzitania group. This being so, we here describe only some of the uses of ideas from the theory of infinite sets in *topology*, the branch that investigates the properties of figures unaffected by very general transformations. All that is required is that these transformations be one-to-one and that they not involve tearing or gluing together.

Initially, topologists studied only figures composed of a finite number of very simple figures called simplexes (points, segments, triangles, tetrahedrons). But later they applied their ideas to more complex sets. And here it became clear that geometric intuition, so faithful a servant in the past, gave incorrect answers to many questions.

The Dutch mathematician Brouwer[40] constructed a number of amazing examples of curves and plane domains. We will now present one of the most surprising of these examples.

Let us draw the map of some country and the countries contiguous to it. Almost every point of the boundary of this country belongs to two and only two countries: the given one and one of its neighbors. At each of these points there are two border guards. On the map there are some points where three countries come together (Figure 30). Three border guards stand at such points. But there is only a finite number of such places on the map. And it seems quite obvious that such points could not occupy the whole boundary of a country, so that there could not be three domains (three countries) sharing the same boundary. In other words, it seems obvious that three border guards from three different countries will not be standing at every point of the boundary.

Figure 31

But Brouwer constructed three such domains. In order to understand his example, imagine an island in the ocean on which there are two lakes with fresh water. One lake is cold and the other is warm. Now we shall carry out the following irrigation project. During the first day we construct canals leading from the ocean and from both lakes in such a way that each canal is "blind" (i.e., is only a creek of the corresponding reservoir), and that the canals nowhere touch one another, so that when we have finished, each point of dry land is at a distance of less than 1 kilometer from sea water and from the water of both lakes (Figure 31).

During the following half day we extend these canals in such a way that they remain "blind" as before and do not touch one another, and so that now the distance from any point of dry land to any of the three canals is less than $\frac{1}{2}$ kilometer. In doing this, of course, the canals have to be made narrower than they were before. In the following quarter day we carry on, arranging matters so that each point of dry land is less than $\frac{1}{4}$ kilometer from any canal, etc. As we continue the process, the canals become ever more winding and narrower. After two days' work the entire island will be permeated by these three canals and converted into a Cantor curve. No matter what point of the curve we stand on, we can scoop up, according to our whim, salt water or warm or cold fresh water. And things are so arranged that the waters do not mix with one another. If we replaced the ocean and lakes by three countries, we would obtain the unusual map we spoke of at the beginning – three border guards, one from each country, would be placed at each point of the boundary.

A "nondissertable" subject. Cantor's definition had one fault– it was not at all suitable for curves in space. And what is a surface in space? No one knew. This problem – to determine what curves and surfaces in space are – was put in the summer of 1921 to his 23-year-old student P.S. Urysohn[41] by the venerable Professor D.F. Yegorov of Moscow University. (It is evident that he gave more thought to the mathematical significance of the problem than to its "dissertability" – this problem was one of the hardest!).

Urysohn quickly comprehended that Yegorov's problem is only a special case of a much more general problem: what is the dimension of a geometric figure, i.e., what are the characteristics of the figure which cause us to say that a segment or a circle has dimension 1, a square has dimension 2, and a cube or a ball has dimension 3? This period in the life of P.S. Urysohn was recalled by his closest friend, a young doctoral candidate in those days and now an academician, the honorary president of the Moscow Mathematical Society, P.S. Aleksandrov, who wrote: "... the whole summer of 1921 was spent in trying to find an 'up-to-date' definition (of dimension); P.S. shifted his interest from one variant to another, constantly setting up examples showing why this or that variant had to be eliminated. He spent two months totally absorbed in his meditations. At last, one morning near the end of August, P.S. awoke with his now well-known inductive definition of dimension in its final form .... That very morning, while we were bathing in the Klayz'ma, P.S. Urysohn told me about his definition of dimension and there, during a conversation that extended over several hours, outlined a plan for a complete theory of dimension composed of a series of theorems, which were then hypotheses that he did not yet know how to go about proving and which were later proved one after another in the months that followed. I never again either participated in or witnessed a mathematical conversation composed of such a dense flow of new ideas as the conversation of that August morning. The whole program outlined then was realized during the winter of 1921/22; by the spring of 1922 the whole theory of dimension was ready ....".

The basic idea of Urysohn's definition of dimension consisted of the following. Two or perhaps several points usually suffice for separating a portion of a curve from the remainder (the part of the four-leafed rose of Figure 32 containing the center can be separated from the rest of the curve by using eight points). But it is already impossible to separate a part of a *surface* from the remainder by removing several points – for this you have to take a complete curve – no matter how many points you take on the surface, it is always possible to go around them. In the same way a surface is needed to separate a part of

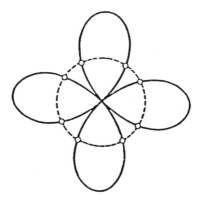

Figure 32

three-dimensional space from the rest of the space.

All this still had to be made more precise: for some curves an infinite set of points has to be removed in order to separate some part, but the totality of these points does not form a curve. Urysohn succeeded in giving a precise formulation of all the definitions required. In a way his definitions are reminiscent of those of Euclid (the ends of a curve are points, the ends of a surface are curves.) But this resemblance is something like the one between the hollowed-out tree trunk of primitive man and a modern ocean liner.

We will make these definitions precise.

Let A be a subset of a set X. A point p of X is called a *boundary point* of A if there are points of A and points of X not in A that are arbitrarily close to p. The *boundary* of A is the set of all its boundary points. For example, the boundary of a square in the plane is its usual boundary and the boundary of that square in space is the square itself.

A set A is *open* in X if it contains none of its boundary points in X. An example of an open set is the interior of a disk in the plane.

A set X has *dimension* 0 if each of its points can be contained in an arbitrarily small set whose boundary in X is empty. Examples of such sets are any finite set, the points with rational coordinates on a straight line, the Cantor set, and so on.

A set X has *dimension* 1 if it is not 0-dimensional and each of its points can be enclosed in an arbitrarily small set open in X whose boundary in X is 0-dimensional.

It turned out that not only all the ordinary curves (circle, line segment,

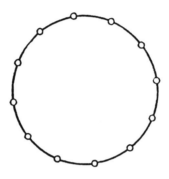

Figure 33

ellipse, etc.) but also all Cantor curves have dimension 1 in Urysohn's sense. Thus, it now became possible to define the notion of a curve in space as well as in the plane, namely, *a curve is a continuum of dimension 1.*

And it was also clear how to define a surface, a 3-dimensional solid, and, in general, a set of any dimension. Since the definition proceeds by numerical order, first defining a set of dimension 0, then a set of dimension 1, then of dimension 2, etc., Urysohn's definition is called *inductive.*

The article should be printed, not reviewed! Urysohn proved many very interesting theorems relating to the notion of dimension that he introduced. But he was unable to find a way to prove one very important theorem; he could not prove that an ordinary cube has dimension 3. After prolonged effort he found a remarkable way out of the difficulty, conceiving a new definition of dimension in the process. We shall not discuss this definition in detail, but shall simply illustrate it with very simple figures.

If we take a segment or a circle, we can divide it into arbitrarily small pieces in such a way that each point belongs to at most two pieces (Figure 33). Here we take the pieces together with their boundaries (i.e., their endpoints). But a square cannot be divided this way. It seems at first glance that if we divide a square into pieces, there will always be points belonging to four pieces (Figure 34a). But if we place the pieces the way bricks are laid in construction, then each point belongs to at most three different pieces (Figure 34b). In the same way, we can divide a cube into small parallelopipeds in such a way that each

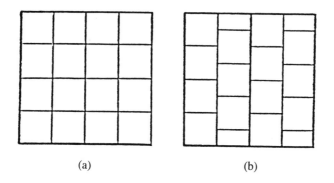

(a)   (b)

Figure 34

point belongs to at most four parallelopipeds.

This is the property that Urysohn took for his new definition of dimension. A figure X is said to have *dimension* n, if n is the smallest nonnegative integer for which the following holds: X can be divided into arbitrarily small closed pieces in such a way that each of its points belongs to at most $n + 1$ different pieces. *

Employing this definition of dimension, Urysohn proved that the dimension of a square is 2, the dimension of a cube is 3, etc. And he then proved that this definition is equivalent to his earlier one.

Urysohn's theory of dimension made a great impression on the mathematical world. This is vividly shown by the following episode. During a trip abroad Urysohn gave a report on his results in Göttingen. Before the rise of the Fascists to power the University of Göttingen was one of the leading mathematical centers. After the report, the head of the Göttingen school of mathematics, David Hilbert, said that the results should be published in *Mathematische Annalen* – one of the most respected mathematical journals of the time. A few months later, Urysohn again gave a report at Göttingen, and Hilbert asked the editor of *Mathematische Annalen*, Richard Courant, whether Urysohn's article had been printed yet. The latter replied that the article was being reviewed. "But I clearly stated that it was to be printed, not reviewed!" Hilbert exclaimed. After such

---

*This definition of dimension goes back to Lebesgue and Brouwer. (Trans.)

an unequivocal declaration the article was soon printed.

For the next three years Urysohn carried on mathematical research unequaled in depth and intensity (during this time he published several dozen articles). A tragic accident abruptly ended his life – he drowned August 17, 1924 while swimming in the Bay of Biscay during a storm. He completed his last mathematical article the day before his death.

After Urysohn's death there still remained numerous rough drafts and outlines of unpublished results. His closest friend (and co-author of many of his articles) P.S. Aleksandrov interrupted his own studies for a time and prepared these articles for publication, thus making these additional results of Urysohn available to all mathematicians. The theory of dimension at present constitutes an important chapter of mathematics.

Chapter 4

In search of the absolute

New complications. The success attained in the study of functions and curves with the help of set theory made it a full and equal member of the family of mathematical sciences. This recognition was acknowledged at the first international congress of mathematicians in Zurich in 1897. Hurwitz[1] and Hadamard,[2] the greatest experts in mathematical analysis, demonstrated in their lectures extremely varied applications of sets and disclosed their connection with the theory of so-called analytic functions. Three years later, at the next international mathematical congress, David Hilbert's list of 23 of the most important unsolved mathematical problems included problems in set theory. In his lecture at the congress Henri Poincaré gave a high rating to Cantor's works. Speaking of the role of intuition and logic in mathematics, he said that mathematics finds in set theory an absolutely permanent and reliable foundation, and now all that remains are the natural numbers and finite or infinite systems of such numbers. In his view, mathematics had become completely arithmetized and, finally, absolutely rigorous.

In view of this high appraisal of set theory by the leading mathematician of the time it is not surprising that academic honors rained upon its creator, Georg Cantor. He was made an honorary member of the London Royal Society, a corresponding member of the Institute of Science, Literature and the Arts in Venice, honorary Doctor of Mathematics of the University of Christiania (now Oslo), and so on.

But every family has its skeleton in the closet. As for mathematics, during the many millennia of its evolution, the skeleton that would pop out of the closet at the most inopportune moments was the inconsistency implicit in the very concept of the infinite. From the moment when Zeno recognized this inconsistency, repeated attempts had been made to restore everything to normal and to make the closet more secure. After the first of these attempts by Eudoxus and Euclid, two millennia passed before Weierstrass and Cantor made the second attempt. We saw that the best mathematicians of that time thought that the attempt had been completely successful. But this time the "skeleton" turned out to be extremely disturbed and popped out of the closet after slightly more than two decades. David Hilbert put the matter in these words:

> What took place was similar to what happened in the evolution of the infinitesimal calculus. Overjoyed by new and rich results, one openly adopted an insufficiently critical attitude concerning the lawfulness of inferences. As a result, contradictions arose, at first rare then progressively more serious, already in connection with the basic formation of concepts and the use of inferences that gradually became routine... Cantor's doctrine was violently attacked from many directions. The countermovement was so impetuous that the most commonly used and most fruitful concepts of mathematics, its simplest and most important inferences were jeopardized and their use was forbidden.

The first sign of trouble in the very foundations of set theory was the paradox, first discovered by Cantor himself in 1895 and published two years later by the Italian mathematician Burali-Forti.[3] At issue was the set of all transfinite numbers. From its definition, this was no worse than any other set, for it seemed to many to be conceivable as a single object. But this set turned out to have an essential flaw. Because it was-well ordered it was describable by some transfinite number Ω. But then Ω must be greater than all transfinite numbers, and thus greater than itself, which is obviously impossible.

Later it became clear that the set of all sets also involves a contradiction. After all, this set must contain all of its subsets. But this is impossible because the cardinality of the set of subsets of any set is greater than the cardinality of that set (see p.67).

Another remarkable example of a specific inconsistent set was published in 1903 by Bertrand Russell.[4] In general, sets do not contain themselves as elements (for example, the set of natural numbers is not a natural number, the set of all triangles is not a triangle, etc.). But there are sets that do contain themselves as elements. For example, the set of all abstract notions is an abstract notion (don't you agree?). Because such sets are rare we'll call them *extraordinary*, and all other sets *ordinary*.

Now let A be the set of all ordinary sets. At first sight there is nothing wrong with this definition; it is not clear why the phrase "the set of all ordinary sets" is worse than the phrase "the set of all triangles." But, in fact, we are faced here with a serious contradiction. Let's try to determine whether A is ordinary or extraordinary. If it is ordinary then it contains itself as an element (remember that A is the set of all ordinary sets). But then, by definition, it is extraordinary. A contradiction. If it is extraordinary, then it must contain itself as an element. But the elements of A are invariably ordinary sets. Again a contradiction. Thus the set A is neither ordinary nor extraordinary.

Such logical contradictions arise in much simpler cases. For example, a soldier was ordered to shave those soldiers and only those soldiers of his platoon who did not shave themselves. The question arose whether he should shave himself. If he shaved himself, then he would be among the group of soldiers who shaved themselves, but he doesn't have the right to shave those soldiers. If he doesn't shave himself, then he belongs to the class of soldiers who do not shave themselves, but then according to the order he has been given he must shave himself.

There are other well-known examples of sets which at first glance appear to be well defined, but turn out on closer inspection to be very poorly defined, and we would be better off saying that these sets are not defined at all. For example, let A be the set of rational numbers which can be defined with the aid of at most two hundred English words (here we include the words "zero," "one," "two," etc.). Since the set of all English words is finite (for simplicity we may assume that we only choose words found in Webster's dictionary and their grammatical derivatives), the set of all such numbers is finite. Suppose that the numbers in question are $r_1, r_2, \ldots, r_N$. Consider the rational number

$$r = 0.n_1 n_2 n_3 \ldots n_N,$$

where n_i is 1 if the ith decimal digit of r_i is different from 1 and 2 otherwise.

The number r differs from r_1 in the first decimal digit, from r_2 in the second decimal digit, and so on. Therefore r does not belong to the set A. But r *must* belong to the set A, because we used less than two hundred words in its definition.

This paradox is closely related to the following one:

What is the smallest integer that cannot be defined by means of a sentence having less than two hundred English words?

Such a number exists since the number of words in the English language is finite; so there must be a number that cannot be defined by means of a sentence having less than two hundred words. And, of course, among these numbers there would have to be a smallest.

On the other hand, this number cannot exist, since its definition involves a contradiction. Indeed, this number is defined by the sentence written above in italics, which we see contains less than two hundred words; while according to its definition this number cannot be determined by such a sentence.

Here is a more complicated example of a finite set of which we cannot decide whether or not it contains a particular element.

We separate all English adjectives into two classes. In the first class we put every adjective which has the property it describes. In the second class we put all the remaining adjectives. For example, "English" belongs in the first class and "German" in the second. Again, "hissing" belongs in the first class and "blue" in the second, as does "monosyllabic."

To distinguish one class from the other we introduce two more adjectives. The adjectives in the first class can all be said to be *autologous* whereas the adjectives in the second class are all *heterologous* (auto = self, hetero = other, logos = sense, law). Clearly, the word *autologous* belongs in the first class. But what of *heterologous*? We leave it to the reader to see that this adjective belongs to neither of the two classes.

These and similar paradoxes can be traced back to the ancient "liar" paradox, ascribed to the Greek philosopher Eubulides of Miletus. It is to the effect that a person who says "I am lying" is neither telling the truth nor lying. (Indeed, if he is telling the truth then he is lying. But if he is lying then he is telling the truth.)

Of course, it would be simplest to say that in set theory one does not consider such whimsical sets. But not giving an exact definition of which sets can be considered and which must be rejected is inviting trouble.

Somehow one problem does not work out. The discovery of paradoxes in set theory made a profound impression on mathematicians. While, for example, Poincaré had only good things to say about Cantor's theory before the publication of the set-theoretic paradoxes, he afterwards spoke of it derisively and maintained that the actually infinite does not exist. After receiving Russell's letter with a description of his paradox, Frege, whose book was just coming off the press, was forced to include in it a remark that, in essence, amounted to crossing out all of its content. The discovery of the paradoxes had an especially painful effect on Cantor. He immersed himself in thoughts of how to eliminate them. He failed, became seriously ill, and gave up scientific work many years before his death. Hilbert exclaimed:

> One must admit that the state we are in now vis-à-vis the paradoxes
> is in the long run unendurable. Just think of it: in mathematics, this
> standard of trustworthiness and truth – the forming of concepts and
> of inferences, as learned, taught, and used by all of us, can lead to
> nonsense. Where is one to find reliability and truth if mathematical
> thought itself can fail?

But in view of the triumphant successes of mathematical analysis based
on set-theoretic conceptions, most mathematicians were initially completely
untroubled by the discovery of paradoxes in Cantor's theory. If there was a
certain unease, then it pertained to the "most distant" areas of mathematics.

What was far more troublesome was the emergence of problems in set
theory that defied solution for a very long time. Many of these problems had to
do with the chasm between the discrete and the continuous, between arithmetic
and geometry – a chasm that seemed to have been surmounted for all time. Of
the two principal cardinalities investigated by Cantor – the countable and the
continual – one derived from arithmetic, from the notion of natural number,
and the other from continuity, from the notion of a continuum. The question
arose how these two cardinalities are related.

It was natural to assume that the cardinality of the continuum is "next"
to the countable cardinality – that is, that there is no uncountable set whose
cardinality is less than that of the continuum. If this hypothesis were true, then
the cardinality of the continuum would be the first transfinite number after all
transfinite numbers of the countable type. The cardinality of the set of countable
transfinite numbers was called *aleph one*, and so the question was whether or
not the cardinality of the continuum is *aleph one*. That it *is* aleph one is the
so-called *continuum hypothesis*, and Cantor pondered over it for many years.
Many times he thought that he had established it but in the end the "solution"
turned out to have been an illusion.

Nor were other scholars more successful in their attempts to prove or disprove the continuum hypothesis. It was number one on Hilbert's list of problems. Luzin pondered it for many years, but in his case too the solution behaved
like a mirage in the desert.

One day a fifteen-year-old boy, Lev Shnirelman[5] was brought in to Luzin.
He was said to possess exceptional mathematical ability – and indeed, he later
became one of the most prominent Soviet mathematicians and a corresponding
member of the Academy of Sciences of the USSR. In order to test the capabili-
ties of this young mathematician Luzin proposed that he solve thirty extremely

difficult problems. He was able to do 29 of the problems. The single unsolved problem was the continuum problem. At the end of a month the young mathematician came back to Luzin and sadly told him: "Somehow one problem doesn't work out."

Having despaired of ever resolving the continuum hypothesis, Luzin used to tell his closest students that he didn't know why the cardinality of the continuum must be aleph one. "Who knows" – he quipped sadly – "maybe it'll turn out to be equal to aleph seventeen."

Then came other problems which also resisted solution in the framework of the usual set theory. They included generalizations and variants of the continuum hypothesis as well as other propositions that could neither be proved nor disproved.

A baffling axiom. The failure to prove the continuum hypothesis gave rise to the question of whether the set of points of an interval can be well-ordered. Put differently, the question was whether or not the scale of transfinite numbers can accommodate the continuum. Cantor was sure that it can. He was convinced that every set can be well-ordered. But in this case too he failed to find a promising approach to the solution of the problem.

An unexpectedly simple and short solution was published in 1904 by Zermelo[6] – he was able to show that any set can be well-ordered. However, Zermelo's proof did not satisfy all mathematicians. The problem was that the proof depended on one assumption which appeared to be far from obvious to both its author and others. This statement came to be called the *axiom of choice* or *Zermelo's axiom* and can be illustrated as follows:

Suppose that in front of you lie several piles of apples. It is obvious that you can select an apple from each pile and put them in a new pile. It would also seem to be true that the same can be done if there are infinitely many apples in each pile as well as infinitely many piles. This is what constitutes the axiom of choice:

If an infinite set of infinite sets is given, then it is possible to choose one element from each set without giving the rule of choice in advance.

Indeed, all the trouble arises from these last words – the axiom of choice leads to completely nonconstructive proofs: with it you can prove, for example, that every set can be well-ordered, but it does not give any information about how to go about it.

Mathematicians employed the axiom of choice for many years, considering it to be completely obvious. But when they began to reflect on it more deeply, it came to appear more and more problematic. Many of the theorems proved with the help of the axiom of choice completely contradict our mathematical intuition. This led Bertrand Russell to speak of this axiom as follows:

"At first it seems obvious, but the more you think about it, the stranger the deductions from this axiom seem to become; in the end you cease to understand what is meant by it."

Luzin admitted: "I ponder Zermelo's axiom day and night. If only someone knew what kind of thing it is."

At this point one reluctantly remembers the words of Mephisto in Goethe's "Faust":

To try to understand it is a wasted effort,
Wise man and fool alike
Are confused
By the sorry mass of contradictions.

True, this axiom did not lead to contradictions but one could obtain from it as many incomprehensible consequences as one wished.

Two apples from one. Let us talk about one of the most surprising consequences of the axiom of choice. Probably everyone has seen a clever magician at work on the stage. First he shows the spectators an empty sack, then he drops a ball into the sack, only to draw out ... two; dropping in the two balls, be pulls out four; dropping in the four, he pulls out eight. Of course, everyone knows that it is no miracle, but is simply "sleight of hand." Such miracles can, however, happen in the theory of sets.

We take an ordinary apple and divide it in any way into four pieces. It seems clear that if we take only two of the pieces, it will not be possible to form an entire apple from them (in the same way, if you have eaten half an orange, you cannot form an entire orange from the remaining slices).

However, mathematicians can divide a ball into five parts in such a way that an entire ball of the same radius can be formed from two of the parts, without supplementing them in any way, simply by translating them as rigid bodies. A second, identical ball can be formed from the other three parts. Thus, we can obtain two distinct balls from the one. It is a pity that this problem is only capable of being solved in theory, otherwise we could make two apples from one, then four, then eight, etc. Of course, the problem cannot be solved in the real world – it would contradict the law of conservation of matter.

But mathematics does not investigate the immediate material world. Rather, it investigates mathematical models of this world. Therefore, if one obtains results that contradict physical intuition, then this is not the fault of mathematics but the consequence of the wrong choice of model.

Thus our strange result, just like some other paradoxical consequences of the axiom of choice, shows only that this axiom must be treated with care. Some mathematicians try to separate sharply assertions derived with the help of this axiom from the others. Dangerous or not, some theorems of mathematical analysis cannot be proved without reliance on this fateful axiom.

A quintet of demons. One of the reasons why the greatest mathematicians refused to believe in the possibility of well-ordering the continuum was the absence of even a hint of a transparent construction for such a well-ordering. In this connection there ensued a spirited discussion of the meaning of the term "there exists" in mathematics. Does this expression mean that an appropriate mathematical object admits a definite construction, or can one also consider sets that exist only on the strength of the axiom of choice? How meaningful is the concept of the set of all subsets of the continuum if we cannot constructively describe most of these subsets? After a certain "period of incubation" the "sickness" came to light, and in 1905 the most famous French mathematicians (Hadamard, Borel, Baire,[7] Lebesgue) published their correspondence on the meaning of infinity and on the question of which infinite sets should be regarded as having existence. These questions also preoccupied Hilbert and the young Dutch mathematician Brouwer.

The participants in the debate disagreed profoundly with one another. In Hilbert's view, the debate was sharp because, beginning with the distant past, no problem troubled the human mind as deeply as that of the nature of the infinite. Almost no other idea influenced human reason in so stimulating and fruitful a manner as the idea of the infinite, and, in Hilbert's view, no other idea required clarification so urgently.

To give the reader an idea of the viewpoints of the participants in this heated debate (small wonder the debate was heated – after all these were mathematical Olympians) we quote a brilliant account taken from Luzin's book *The present state of the theory of functions of a real variable*. In it he makes use of variants of "Maxwell's demon."[*] Luzin wrote:

---

[*]Maxwell's demon made heat flow from a cold to a warm region by opening and closing a

If we analyze the views of the creators of the modern theory of functions, then we can easily notice that each of them adopts in the course of his work a definite conception of what is possible and admissible. Its bounds are the bounds of mathematics and beyond them begins a domain that lies – to use Borel's term – outside mathematics. . . If, following Maxwell's example, we assign each author's domain of the possible and realizable to the appropriate imaginary creature, then we get the following scheme.

1. Brouwer's "demon." His domain is the finite with a specified finite upper bound. All beyond this domain is "outside mathematics."

2. Baire's "demon." His domain is simply the domain of the finite without the prescription of a finite upper bound. The infinite is merely a *façon de parler* and is "outside mathematics."

3. Borel's "demon." His domain is the domain of the countably infinite. Every uncountable set is "outside mathematics."

4. Lebesgue's "demon." His domain is the domain of the cardinality of the continuum. Every operation that requires a continuum of simple steps is available to this "demon.". . .

5. Zermelo's "demon." His field of operations extends to all cardinalities. In particular, Zermelo's demon can well-order every set.

The following example illustrates the difference between the respective strengths of the Borel demon and of the Lebesgue demon. Suppose that we wish to find out if the inequality $x \leq a$ holds for all elements of a set X. If X is countable, then Borel's demon can solve the problem because he must verify just countably many inequalities $x_k \leq a$. If X has the cardinality of the continuum, then Borel's demon can't solve the problem but Lebesgue's demon can.

Luzin's own view of these matters was ambiguous. For the most part he shared Borel's position, noting that "the concept of an uncountable infinity is purely negative and has no objective reality whatsoever; it is a concept due only to man's ability to devise proofs 'by contradiction' and does not correspond to any attainable reality. . . " At other times he tended more to Baire's viewpoint and maintained that we lack a sufficiently clear conception of the actual infinite even though this concept can be defined in terms of abstract logic. To the Polish

---

hole in a diaphragm that divided a gas-filled vessel into two halves A and B. The demon would open the hole to let a fast molecule pass from A to B and close it otherwise. (Translator)

mathematician Kuratowski[8] he wrote: "No matter what, I cannot consider the set of positive integers as given, for the very concept of the actual infinite strikes me as insufficiently natural to consider it by itself." And further: "The fundamental problem is to explain whether or not the sequence of positive integers is completely objective. It seems that it is almost objective and that there are [in it] traces of unquestionable subjectivity, so that it is impossible to speak of the sequence of positive integers at all times, in all cases, in one and the same sense." He thought that it was too early to formulate the burning problem of the uniqueness of the sequence of positive integers and to speak of finite numbers that are inaccessible if we start with 1.

Bourbaki's[9] viewpoint of the essence of mathematical problems is the very opposite of Luzin's. He claims that whatever is free of contradictions exists, and so shares Zermelo's position. This means that he admits arbitrary cardinalities, and accepts without reservation the axiom of choice and all its consequences, including the paradoxical subdivision of the sphere and the claim of the well-orderedness of the continuum. He seems to take no interest whatever in the question of the possible applicability of such a mathematics to the problem of knowing the real world.

P.S. Aleksandrov also approved of working with sets of arbitrary cardinality. For example, he extended the concept of dimension to a very large set of spaces that satisfy no countability conditions, developed geometry in such spaces, and so on. Thus Zermelo's demon enables one to obtain extremely beautiful results but, on the other hand, leads to assertions whose meaning cannot be grasped by intuition.

What complicates the choice of one of the five demons listed earlier is that the "unpleasantnesses" that arise in connection with sets of arbitrary cardinality can be modeled in countable sets. It follows that the blame for the complications that arise in mathematics must be laid at the door not of sets of too high cardinality but of the idea of the actual infinite.

Banishing the infinite. David Hilbert embarked on a bold and profound attempt to resolve the difficulties of the theory of infinite sets. He would not give up the achievements of this theory (he put it in a colorful phrase: "No one will banish us from the paradise created for us by Cantor"). In his work *On the infinite* Hilbert noted that while the infinitely small and infinitely large had once been removed from mathematical analysis, the infinite managed to elbow its way back in, first through the infinite sequences used to define real numbers and then in the real numbers thought of as a completed set.

Weierstrass had reduced the concepts of the infinitely small and the infinitely large to inequalities involving finite magnitudes. Similarly, Hilbert wanted to eliminate infinite sets from mathematics. In his view, the use of such sets in mathematical arguments should be regarded as a *façon de parler* that makes it possible to briefly describe complex properties of finite sets. The infinite is inadmissible as the basis of rational thought because it is not part of nature. That was a reflection of Hilbert's notion of the harmony between existence and thought. In his view, the road to reliable operation with the infinite led through the finite.

This is the *finitary* viewpoint. To realize it rigorously Hilbert gave a restricted list of admissible symbols. To guard mathematics against the intrusion of notions of the infinite connected with visual appeal and the use of intuition he elaborated a theory of formal proofs. In it, symbols that express logical assertions are transformed by means of rigorously formulated rules in a manner similar to that used in algebra.

The first stated aim of the new calculus was a formal proof of the consistency of the arithmetic of positive integers. For more than two decades Hilbert and his students looked for a road to the solution of this problem. They achieved many "intermediate" successes but the final triumph eluded them.

In 1931 there appeared a paper of Kurt Gödel[10] that was like a bolt from the blue. By sophisticated refinement and formalization of arguments that went back in essence to the "liar" paradox, Gödel proved the astounding result that in any formal system that includes the arithmetic of the natural numbers it is possible to formulate an undecidable proposition – that is, a statement that can neither be proved nor disproved. At the same time, if one accepts the existence of the complete set of natural numbers, then this statement is true or false. Thus Borel's demon, capable of carrying out countably many checks, could find out which of the two possibilities holds.

Gödel's result was one of the greatest achievements of logic in the more than two thousand years of its existence. (Once, to be sure, he happened to hear, at a conference on logic, a lecture that claimed that nothing had been achieved in logic since Aristotle's time!) His discovery brought to light the chasm between the true and the provable. We shall not go into the circle of problems connected with Gödel's discovery but will refer the reader to the splendid [Russian] book *The provable and the unprovable* by Yu. I. Manin, published in 1979 by Soviet Radio.

While Gödel's proof showed that Hilbert's program can not be realized, his efforts were not wasted. His investigations gave rise to *metamathematics*, a new branch of mathematics devoted to proof theory. This led to a great deepening of ideas and to the evolution of the methods of mathematical logic. Later, all this turned out to be of great use for the elaboration of algorithmic languages for computers.

Axiomatization of the infinite. Another path toward overcoming the difficulties in the theory of infinite sets was chosen by mathematicians who tried to base it on a system of axioms. One such system was proposed in 1908 by Zermelo and later refined by A. Fraenkel. The Zermelo-Fraenkel system describes the properties of the relation of belonging, $x \in y$, which is used to define the relation of inclusion, $x \subset y$, for sets and the notion of equality of sets. Axioms are formulated that assert that two sets containing the same elements are equal, and that equal sets are contained in the same sets. Then come axioms that codify the rules for set building – the forming of a pair of sets and of the union of an arbitrary set of sets. Then there is an axiom that asserts the existence of the set of subsets of a set. Another axiom in this group is the rule that singles out a subset of a set on the basis of certain properties of its elements. This axiom eliminates the paradoxical sets of Cantor, Burali-Forti and Russell. All these sets were given by properties of their elements but were not subsets of some "lawful" set.

These axioms enable one to prove the existence of the empty set and to obtain from any set x a new set $\{x\}$ whose only element is x. Of course, the Zermelo-Fraenkel system includes the axiom of choice. It also includes an axiom which says that the image of a set under some mapping is also a set. Finally, the system contains "the axiom of the infinite" which, in essence, asserts the existence of the infinite set of natural numbers (although this concept does not appear in the statement of the axiom).

The two critical questions facing any system of axioms are: is it possible to deduce from it two assertions that contradict one another, and can one prove or disprove all assertions formulated by means of its terms. The adherents of the Zermelo-Fraenkel system feel that it must be consistent (that is free of contradictions) because no contradictions have turned up thus far (they may, of course, turn up in the future). To test its power, attempts were made to use it to prove or disprove the continuum hypothesis. But here some remarkable results were found.

It all began with a discovery Gödel made in 1939. By adjoining the continuum hypothesis to the axioms of set theory Gödel obtained a consistent system (of course, this consistency is relative; it is predicated on the assumption that the axioms of set theory are consistent). Luzin had earlier anticipated the paradoxical possibility that the axioms of set theory contradict neither the continuum hypothesis nor its negation. In 1963 Paul Cohen[11] showed that this is indeed the case. He proved that one can not deduce the continuum hypothesis from the Zermelo-Fraenkel system of axioms. Also, it turned out that the axiom of choice is independent of the remaining axioms of the Zermelo-Fraenkel system, much as the parallel axiom cannot be proved or disproved on the basis of the remaining axioms of geometry. It also became clear that it is possible, without contradiction, to adjoin to the system of axioms obtained from the Zermelo-Fraenkel system by replacing the axiom of choice by its negation the assertion of the impossiblity of well-ordering the continuum. At virtually the same time as Cohen, the Czech mathematician P. Vopenka obtained similar (and even stronger) results.

The situation in mathematics that resulted from the publication of the papers by Gödel, Cohen and Vopenka was similar to that in geometry after the publication of the works of Lobachevski and J. Bolyai.[12] But Euclidean and non-Euclidean geometry were regarded as different mathematical models of the real world, and the choice between the two affected physics and not mathematics. The discovery of hyperbolic geometry did not impinge on the foundations of mathematics. But now it is precisely the foundations of mathematics that are involved. Now a mathematician can choose the set theory he prefers. He can choose the set theory in which the axiom of choice and the continuum hypothesis hold, or the set theory in which one rejects the axiom of choice and the possibility of well-ordering the continuum. He can also choose other possibilities, for example, to accept the axiom of choice but to reject the continuum hypothesis. In the latter case he must assume that the continuum has a place on the scale of transfinite numbers but its place on that scale is unknown.

If one bears in mind that set theory claims to be the basis of mathematics, then there are many mathematics, and it is up to the individual mathematician to choose among them. Of course, each mathematics yields its model of the real world, but the differences among them are deep and touch on the most fundamental questions of the theory of cognition. It is safe to assume that had Hilbert lived to read Cohen's papers, he would have taken back his proud words:

> Mathematics is a science without hypotheses. To justify it, I don't need, like Kronecker, the Lord God, or, like Poincaré, the assumption of the special ability of reason based on the principle of mathematical induction, or, like Brouwer, primary intuition, or, finally, like Russell and Whitehead,[13] the axioms of infinity, reduction

and completeness, which are genuine hypotheses of a substantial nature, and, in addition, completely improbable.

A modern mathematician is much more likely to approve of the viewpoint of the noted American mathematician and logician Willard Quine:[14]

> Beginning in 1901, there have appeared many set theories none of which is indisputably superior to the others. Even the question of whether they are free of individual contradictions is debatable in the setting of such an examination, because we can no longer rely on common sense when establishing the likelihood of various propositions. Set theory is discredited by paradoxes and as a foundation for mathematics it is far less reliable than its superstructure. It is therefore clear that we cannot regard set theory as the foundation of mathematics and hope that it will deliver us from the fear of unsoundness of classical mathematics. In developing all possible systems we try to find a scheme that would reproduce in the corresponding superstructure the accepted laws of classical mathematics. At this stage we regard set theory as a convenient short dictionary of mathematical terms used for the formulation of the common system of axioms of classical mathematics.

We conclude this section with Kolmogorov's relevant opinion:

> The clarification of the question to what extent, and under what conditions, it is admissible, in the study of infinite sets, to ignore their process of formation, cannot as yet be regarded as complete.

A lost bet. It remains to tell of an attempt to take set theory, and so all of mathematics, out of its state of prolonged crisis. This was undertaken in 1907 by Brouwer, who relied to significant extent on the oft-repeated opinions of Kronecker and Poincaré. According to Brouwer and his followers, the special character of the concept of the infinite was completely ignored in analysis and in geometry from the 17th century onwards. Thus, the presumably rigorous methods of the theory of real numbers and of mathematical analysis, introduced into mathematics by scholars in the 19th century, not only failed to achieve their aim but led to the creation of an elaborate system based on the completely false tendency to deal with the infinite using means developed for finite sets. This view spelled total rejection of the conception of mathematics that went back to Cauchy, Weierstrass and Cantor.

Brouwer and his school believed that this conception of real number and of function masks the dangers that lurk in the concept of the infinite, abounds in vicious circles, and lays claim to an extraordinary generality that inevitably leads to contradictions. This view was tantamount to complete rejection of the 19th century's progress in strengthening the foundations of classical mathematics. In particular, Brouwer and his school viewed Cantor's set theory as "an interesting pathological special case" in the history of mathematics that would likely cause grief to future generations. What was especially interesting in all this is that Brouwer had to his credit significant achievements in set-theoretic mathematics.

To set mathematics on what they regarded as the right path it was necessary to rely on intuition, hence the name *intuitionism* for this school of thought. The intuitionists rejected the idea of the continuum as a point set because they regarded the idea of the continuum as prior to the idea of a point. They said that the continuum is the medium for free formation of points and not a point set.

The intuitionists subjected to withering criticism the logic used by mathematicians in the 19th century and earlier. In particular, they categorically rejected the law of the excluded middle, one of the fundamental laws of Aristotelian logic, which asserts that every proposition is either true or false. They argued that this law was inferred from observations on finite sets of objects and applies only to such sets. For example, to establish the truth of the proposition: "Among the people living on the Earth on 1 January 1983 none is 200 years old" it suffices to check the age of everyone alive on that day. But this method of verification cannot be used to determine the properties of elements of infinite sets. The elements of such a set cannot be lined up for a check of documents.

This meant that the "arsenal" of the intuitionists lacked so powerful a tool as proof by contradiction. They rejected "pure existence proofs" and required in each case a presentation of a concrete example of an object with given properties. Thus, they would accept as an existence proof of an object only a description of a construction of that object. Hermann Weyl, who joined the camp of the intuitionists, compared concrete assertions to treasures and existence proofs to documents containing instructions for finding them.

In other words, the intuitionists required a transition from assertions of the form "there exist even numbers" to assertions of the form "2 is an even number."

In a lecture on intuitionism Brouwer gave the following example of an assertion that can neither be proved nor disproved: "In the decimal representation of the number π there are ten nines in a row." At that time the number of known digits in the expansion of π was 707 (many of which turned out to be incorrect). Computers have enabled us to find a great many more digits of the decimal expansion of π, so that among them there are, possibly, ten nines in a row. But if the number ten is replaced by 10^{1000}, then all attempts at verification of our hypothesis are forever doomed, the speed of future computers notwithstanding. Since the problem admits of no theoretical solution, it follows that the assertion about the existence of 10^{1000} nines in the decimal expansion of π is necessarily unverifiable. Incidentally, one of the mathematicians present at Brouwer's lecture remarked that while we don't know whether the assertion is true or not the Lord God knows. "I have no direct contact with God" was Brouwer's dry retort.

The intuitionists changed mathematics in radical ways. Their analysis contains no discontinuous functions. In their arithmetic, the fact that a product is zero does not directly imply that one of its factors is zero. Almost every assertion of classical mathematics must be replaced by a strange-sounding intuitionistic analogue, and much had to be given up. "I don't regard any of the theorems in the usual textbooks as inviolable" declared the intuitionist Skolem.

The call to so radical a transformation won the approval of only a small – but very influential – group of scholars. Hilbert was a fierce opponent of Brouwer's reform. He said: "What Weyl and Brouwer are doing is none other than a revival of Kronecker's idea. They try to save mathematics by tossing overboard all that provokes concern... They crumble and chop science. If we accepted the reform they propose, then we would be running the risk of losing the greatest part of our precious treasures."

Hilbert angrily asserted that taking away from mathematicians the law of the excluded middle was the same as depriving astronomers of telescopes or forbidding boxers to use their fists. He wrote that the prohibition of existence proofs and of the law of the excluded middle is almost synonymous with a repudiation of mathematical science, and the sorry remnants, the few, incomplete and unrelated results worked out by intuitionists, cannot compare with the power of modern mathematics. Hilbert complained bitterly that the hypnotic power of a single temperamental and clever man could have so unbelievable and eccentric an influence on the mathematical milieu.

The intuitionists did not leave Hilbert's strictures unanswered; they claimed that his program for saving mathematics was bound to banish from it all meaning. But the majority of mathematicians sided with Hilbert. They felt that the very existence of mathematics and the vast scope of its applications prove that it is neither absurd nor empty, and to cure a toe one need not amputate the leg.

In spite of the fact that most mathematicians rejected the ideas of the intuitionists, the latter were sure of their future victory. In 1918 Hermann Weyl bet his friend George Pólya[15] that in 20 years the ideas of the intuitionists would triumph. As a criterion, he indicated two theorems of classical analysis that can be found in every textbook of higher mathematics but are meaningless in intuitionistic mathematics. He thought that within 20 years these theorems would vanish from generally accepted mathematics. But after 20 years Weyl admitted that he'd lost the bet.

We note that in the last few decades interest in intuitionism has again been on the increase and many eminent logicians have explicitly or implicitly joined this trend in mathematical thought.

Conclusion

We have finished our journey along the meandering road taken by the human mind in its attempt to master that most contradictory of concepts, infinity, to tame it and use it to apprehend reality. First there were the myths. Then came the first scientific quests of Pythagoras, Zeno and Aristotle. By now mankind has attained such impressive achievements as the modern cosmological theories, the intricate constructions of mathematical analysis, and the theory of infinite-dimensional spaces.

In some of these creations of the human mind one is almost unaware of the complexity of the underlying conceptions. While carrying out in the course of technical computations the usual operations of differentiation and integration of functions, the engineer does not stop to think that there was a time when these operations were viewed as virtually unattainable. As Engels put it:

> When variable magnitudes entered mathematics and when their variability was extended to the infinitely small and infinitely large, then mathematics, usually so very moral, perpetrated the Fall: it ate the apple of knowledge and this opened for it the road to gigantic achievements but also to delusions. The virgin state of absolute meaningfulness, of irrefutable provability of all things mathematical ... belonged to the past. An era of discord had arrived.

Now these words seem almost like prophetic anticipations of the modern state of the investigations of the deep problems of the theory of infinite sets.

The reader of this book must have more than once asked himself the question of the practical value of the quests it describes, of the possible practical applicability of cardinalities of infinite sets, transfinite numbers, unusual functions and curves from the mathematical hall of wonders, and so on. This is the most difficult question in the majority of scientific investigations. It was for a good reason that Michael Faraday said to some lord who wanted to know the practical value of electromagnetic researches: "And what can one say of the future of a newborn baby?" At one time or another genetics, relativity theory and quantum physics were accused of being out of touch with the real world. Many regarded Tsiolkovski's idea of interplanetary voyages as just a dream.

When trying to answer the question of the practical value of set-theoretic investigations one must keep in mind that set theory has three essentially different aspects: operations on sets, cardinalities of infinite sets, and the set-theoretic approach to mathematics as a whole. The roots of the first of these aspects reach back to the distant past; indeed, in essence, Aristotle's syllogisms express definite relations between sets and operations on them. Set-theoretic operations are indispensable if, say, computers are to do their job of collecting and processing data, and such operations are therefore provided for in algorithmic languages. We need hardly mention the widespread use of symbols for such operations in modern mathematical literature – it would be hopeless to try to rewrite many classical works of 20th-century mathematics without using the symbols for inclusion, and union and intersection of sets.

The question of the practical significance of the theory of infinite sets is more difficult. Its role is rather indirect, in the sense that set-theoretic concepts underlie many frequently used mathematical theorems. Relevant examples are fixed-point theorems that are the basis for many computational schemes, the theorem of the compactness of the product of compact spaces, and so on. One of the most important concepts of modern mathematics, that of infinite-dimensional Hilbert space, arose out of Hilbert's investigations in the theory of systems of equations with infinitely many unknowns. The most important model of such a space consists of discontinuous functions that can be integrated only in the sense of the Lebesgue integral. It is also in Hilbert space that we find a most remarkable construct – the Wiener spiral, whose directions at any two of its points are orthogonal. Its strangeness notwithstanding, this spiral is the geometric image of stochastic processes with independent increments, a concept of importance for applications of probability theory.

We must not forget that the conceptions of mathematical logic that play such an important role in the theory of algorithmic languages were to a large extent created in connection with attempts to resolve the paradoxes that arose in the theory of infinite sets. In recent years, other aspects of this theory have begun to acquire practical value. Thus the well-known American applied mathematician Richtmayer thinks that concepts derived in part from set theory are likely to become part of everyday practice in physics. He is also of the opinion that every area of mathematics is of potential interest for physics.

The most contentious aspect of set theory is the attempt to construct all mathematics on a set-theoretic base (the so-called "bourbakism"). Many scholars hold radically different views on this issue. Some feel that this attempt makes possible a unified treatment of different mathematical problems as well as the application of methods developed for the solution of problems of one kind to the study of seemingly unrelated problems. Other mathematicians, (usually closely connected with the applied side of the subject) accuse this approach of being riddled with unnecessary formalism and regard the tools used as incompatible with the problems under study. These disagreements are due to the divergence of the worldviews of the opposing sides and of their different estimates of the importance of various problems and achievements of mathematics. The truth may turn out to be some dialectic synthesis of the now diametrically opposite views.

The outcome of these disagreements notwithstanding, the rise and evolution of set theory was one of the most important stages in the history of mathematics and in mankind's attempt to master the concept of the infinite. This process will never end, for the idea of the infinite is inexhaustible and the human mind will forever find in it new aspects.

Notes

Chapter 1

1. Thales of Miletus (c. 625-547 BC). Ancient Greek mathematician and astronomer. The first to introduce the notion of proof into mathematics. Proved some very simple geometric theorems.

2. Anaximander of Miletus (c. 585-525 BC). Ancient Greek philosopher. Student of Thales. First to make the conjecture about the infinity of worlds and of the universe.

3. Weyl, Hermann (1885-1955). German mathematician. Author of important works on mathematical analysis, differential geometry, algebra and number theory. Interested in the philosophy of mathematics. One of the founders of intuitionism.

4. Leucippus (c. 500-440 BC). Ancient Greek philosopher, atomist.

5. Epicurus (c. 341-271 BC). Ancient Greek philosopher, atomist.

6. Zeno of Elea (c. 490-430BC). Ancient Greek philosopher and author of paradoxes that constituted a critique of notions such as multiplicity, infinity, motion, and (a naive view of) the continuum.

7. Diogenes of Samos (413-323 BC). Ancient Greek philosopher.

8. Fraenkel, Abraham (1891-1965). German mathematician. Author of works on mathematical logic.

9. Naan, Gustav Ivanovich (b. 1919). Soviet philosopher. Interested in the philosophy of science.

10. Antiphon (second half of the fifth century BC). Ancient Greek philosopher-sophist.

11. Eudoxus of Cnidos (c. 408- c. 355 BC). Ancient Greek mathematician and astronomer, author of a theory of incommensurable magnitudes and of the "method of exhaustion" for proving theorems on areas and volumes.

12. Hypatia of Alexandria (370-415). Philosopher, mathematician and astronomer. Lynched by a fanatical Christian mob incited by bishop Cyril of Alexandria.

13. Albert the Great (c. 1193-1280). German philosopher, naturalist, theologian and logician. Attempted to adapt Aristotle's teachings to theology.

14. Bradwardine, Thomas (1300-1349). English mathematician, author of *Tractatus de continuo*. First to use the word "irrational" in a mathematical sense.

15. Baconthorpe, John. English scholastic of the 14th century.

16. Cusa, Nicholas (1401-1464). German philosopher and theologian. His works prepared the ground for Renaissance pantheism and created premises for the justification of the notion of infiniteness of the Universe.

17. Cavalieri, Bonaventura (1598-1647). Italian mathematician, student of Galileo, and author of a method of indivisibles for finding areas and volumes.

18. Fontenelle, Bernard (1657-1757). French author and popularizer of science. One of the pioneers of the philosophy of the Enlightenment.

19. D'Alembert, Jean (1717-1783). French mathematician, mechanician and philosopher. One of the creators of mathematical physics.

20. Abel, Niels (1802-1829). Norwegian mathematician. Proved the unsolvability in radicals of the general quintic. One of the creators of the modern criteria of rigor in mathematical analysis.

21. Cauchy, Augustin-Louis (1789 - 1857). French mathematician. Author of the theory of functions of a complex variable. Developed mathematical analysis based on the limit concept.

22. Gauss, Carl (1777-1855). The greatest German mathematician of the 19th century. Obtained many fundamental results in algebra, geometry, number theory, and mathematical analysis.

23. Schumacher, Heinrich (1780-1850). German astronomer.

24. Riemann, Bernhard (1826-1866). German mathematician. Obtained many outstanding results in the theory of functions of a complex variable, in geometry, and in other areas of mathematics. One of the creators of the concept of a multidimensional space (Riemannian geometry).

25. Lobachevski, Nikolai Ivanovich (1792-1856). Russian mathematician. Creator of non-Euclidean geometry.

26. Fridman (Friedmann), Aleksandr Aleksandrovich (1888-1925). Soviet physicist and cosmologist.

27. Lemaître, Georges (1894-1966). Belgian astronomer and astrophysicist. Author of the theory of an expanding Universe.

28. Sitter, Willem de (1872-1934). Dutch astronomer. Pioneered the application of relativity theory to cosmology.

29. Slipher, Vesto (1875-1969). American astronomer. First to measure radial velocities of galaxies.

30. Hubble, Edwin (1889-1953). American astronomer. Showed that galaxies are systems of stars.

31. Doroshkevich, Andrei Georgievich (b. 1937). Soviet physicist and cosmologist.

32. Novikov, Igor Dmitrievich (b. 1935). Soviet astrophysicist and cosmologist.

33. Brillouin, Leon (1889-1969). French physicist. Author of works on quantum mechanics, information theory, and philosophy of science.

34. Zelmanovich, Abram Leonidovich (b. 1913). Soviet cosmologist.

Chapter 2

1. Cantor, Georg (1845-1918). German mathematician. Creator of set theory.

2. Luzin, Nikolai Nikolaievich (1883-1950). Soviet mathematician. One of the founders of the Moscow mathematical school. Author of a number of distinguished works on set theory and the theory of functions of a real variable.

3. Manin, Yuri Ivanovich (b. 1937). Soviet mathematician. Author of works on algebra and the applications of mathematics to modern physics.

4. Zadeh, Lotfi (b. 1918). American mathematician. Author of the theory of fuzzy sets.

5. Dirichlet, Lejeune (1805-1859). German mathematician. Author of works on number theory, mathematical physics and the theory of series.

6. Dedekind, Richard (1831-1916). German mathematician. One of the creators of modern algebra. In his works Dedekind came close to the ideas of set theory.

7. Bolzano, Bernard (1781-1848). Czech mathematician, philosopher and logician. Author of a number of works on the foundations of mathematical analysis and the theory of infinite sets.

8. Bernstein, Felix (1878-1956). German mathematician.

9. Liouville, Joseph (1809-1882). French mathematician. Author of works on mathematical analysis and number theory.

10. Lindeman, Carl (1852-1939). German mathematician. Proved that π is transcendental.

11. Aleksandrov, Pavel Sergeevich (1896-1982). Soviet mathematician. Founder of the Soviet school of topology.

12. Kolmogorov, Andrei Nikolaevich (1903-1987). Soviet mathematician. Author of many outstanding works on functions of a real variable, the theory of probability and topology.

Chapter 3

1. Descartes, René (1596-1650). French mathematician and philosopher. Created analytic geometry, introduced the notion of a variable and studied relations between variables.

2. Weierstrass, Carl (1815-1897). German mathematician. One of the creators of the theory of functions of a complex variable. Created an arithmetical theory of real numbers and based on it a restructured account of mathematical analysis.

3. Méray, Charles (1835-1911). French mathematician. Created an arithmetical theory of real numbers at the same time as Weierstrass.

4. Frege, Gottlob (1848-1925). German mathematician and logician.

5. Hilbert, David (1862-1943). The greatest German mathematician of the 20th century. Author of outstanding works in the following areas: the theory of invariants, the theory of algebraic numbers, the calculus of variations, the foundations of mathematics, and functional analysis. Introduced the concept of an infinite-dimensional space.

6. Kronecker, Leopold (1823-1891). German mathematician who worked in the areas of algebra and number theory.

7. Napier, John (1550-1617). Scottish mathematician. Created the theory of logarithms.

8. Bernoulli, Johann (1667-1748). Swiss mathematician. One of the founders of mathematical analysis. Contributed substantially to the evolution of the concept of function.

9. Euler, Leonhard (1707-1783). Mathematician, physicist, mechanician and astronomer. Born in Switzerland. Spent most of his life in Russia. Author of outstanding works in analysis in which he developed general methods of integration and of solution of differential equations. Studied functions of a complex variable.

10. Bernoulli, Daniel (1700-1782). Physicist and mathematician. Son of Johann Bernoulli. Author of a number of works on mathematical physics.

11. Fourier, Joseph (1768-1830). French mathematician. Studied equations of mathematical physics and made extensive use of trigonometric series for their solution.

12. Poincaré, Henri (1854-1912). French mathematician, physicist, astronomer and philosopher. One of the greatest mathematicians of the 20th century. Author of outstanding works in almost all areas of mathematics.

13. Von Koch, Helge (1870-1924). Swedish mathematician. His work on infinite systems of linear equations prepared the ground for functional analysis.

14. Hermite, Charles (1822-1901). French mathematician. Author of numerous investigations in mathematical analysis, algebra, and number theory.

15. Stieltjes, Thomas (1856-1894). Dutch mathematician. Author of a number of works in mathematical analysis.

16. Perrin, Jean (1870-1942). French physicist and physical chemist. Made experimental studies of Brownian motion.

17. Wiener, Norbert (1894-1964). American scholar, "father of cybernetics." A number of his works are devoted to functional analysis and the study of infinite-dimensional spaces.

18. Lagrange, Joseph (1736-1813). French mathematician and mechanician. One of the creators of the calculus of variations, author of a number of works on mathematical analysis and its applications.

19. Jordan, Camille (1838-1922). French mathematician. One of the founders of group theory.

20. Peano, Giuseppe (1858-1932). Italian mathematician. Studied the theory of differential equations and formal-logical foundations of mathematics.

21. Borel, Émile (1871-1956). French mathematician. Author of works in the area of functions of a real variable and in many other areas of mathematical analysis.

22. Lebesgue, Henri (1875-1941). French mathematician. Introduced a generalization of the notion of integral that is widely used in modern mathematics.

23. Schwartz, Hermann (1843-1921). German mathematician. Author of works in the area of mathematical analysis.

24. Darboux, Gaston (1842-1917). French mathematician. Author of works on differential geometry, the theory of differential equations, and other areas of mathematics.

25. Ostrogradski, Mikhail Vasil'evich (1801-1862). Russian mathematician. One of the founders of the St. Petersburg school of mathematics. Author of outstanding works on the equations of mathematical physics, mathematical analysis, and theoretical mechanics.

26. Chebyshev, Pafnuti L'vovich (1821-1894). Russian mathematician and mechanician. Founder of the St. Petersburg school of mathematics, author of outstanding works on mathematical analysis, number theory, the theory of probability, and the theory of mechanisms.

27. Markov, Andrei Andreevich (1856-1922). Russian mathematician. Author of outstanding works on number theory, mathematical analysis, and probability theory.

28. Lyapunov, Aleksandr Mikhailovich (1857-1918). Russian mathematician and mechanician. Author of outstanding works dealing with potential theory, stability of motion, the theory of equilibrium of rotating fluids, and probability.

29. Steklov, Vladimir Andreevich (1864-1926). Russian and Soviet mathematician. Author of outstanding works on mathematical physics.

30. Korkin, Aleksandr Nikolaevich (1837-1908). Russian mathematician. Author of works on number theory and on partial differential equations.

31. Zhegalkin, Ivan Ivanovich (1869-1947). Soviet mathematician. Author of works on mathematical logic, the foundations of mathematics, and set theory.

32. Egorov, Dmitri Fedorovich (1869-1931). Soviet mathematician. Author of works on differential geometry, the theory of integral equations, and the theory of functions of a real variable.

33. Men'shov, Dmitri Eugenevich (b. 1892). Soviet mathematician. Author of outstanding works on trigonometric and orthogonal series.

34. Bari, Nina Karlovna (1901-1961). Soviet mathematician. Author of works on trigonometric series.

35. Suslin, Mikhail Yakovlevich (1894-1919). Russian mathematician. One of the creators of descriptive set theory.

36. Novikov, Petr Sergeevich (1901-1975). Soviet mathematician. Author of outstanding works on descriptive set theory and mathematical logic.

37. Keldysh, Liudmila Vsevolodovna (1904-1976). Soviet mathematician. Author of works on descriptive set theory.

38. Sierpiński, Waclaw (1882-1969). Polish mathematician. Founder of the Polish school of mathematics. Author of works on the theory of functions of a real variable, topology, and number theory.

39. Lavrent'ev, Mikhail Alekseevich (1900-1980). Soviet mathematician and mechanician. One of the founders of the Siberian branch of the Academy of Science of the USSR. Author of outstanding works on the theory of functions, quasiconformal mappings, aero and hydrodynamics.

40. Brouwer, Luitzen (1881-1966). Dutch mathematician. Author of important results in topology, functional analysis, and mathematical physics.

41. Urysohn, Paul Samuilovich (1898-1924). Soviet mathematician. Author of important works in the area of general topology and one of the creators of general dimension theory.

Chapter 4

1. Hurwitz, Adolf (1859-1919). German mathematician. Author of works in mathematical analysis, the theory of functions, algebra, and number theory.

2. Hadamard, Jacques (1865-1963). French mathematician. Author of outstanding works in the area of mathematical physics, the theory of functions, and number theory.

3. Burali-Forti, Cesaro (1861-1931). Italian mathematician.

4. Russell, Bertrand (1872-1970). English logician, philosopher, mathematician and social activist. Founder of logicism.

5. Shnirelman, Lev Henrikhovich (1905-1938). Soviet mathematician. Author of outstanding works in number theory, topology, and topological and quantitative methods of mathematical analysis.

6. Zermelo, Ernst (1871-1953). German mathematician. Author of works on set theory, the calculus of variations, and probability theory.

7. Baire, René (1874-1932). French mathematician. Worked in the area of the theory of functions of a real variable.

8. Kuratowski, Kazimierz (1896-1980). Polish mathematician. Author of works in the area of topology, the theory of fu₁ ctions of a real variable, and mathematical logic.

9. Bourbaki, Nicolas. Pseudonym of a group of modern French mathematicians who have published a treatise of many volumes titled *The elements of mathematics*.

10. Gödel, Kurt (1906-1978). Abstract mathematician and logician.

11. Cohen, Paul (b. 1934). American mathematician. Proved the independence of the continuum hypothesis.

12. Bolyai, János (1802-1860). Hungarian mathematician. Created hyperbolic geometry shortly after Lobachevski and independently of him.

13. Whitehead, Alfred (1861-1947). English mathematician and logician. Coauthor (with B. Russell) of *Principia mathematica*.

14. Quine, Willard (b. 1908). American mathematician. One of the greatest experts in mathematical logic and the foundations of mathematics.

15. Pólya, George (1887-1985). Hungarian mathematician. Author of works on functional analysis, mathematical statistics, and combinatorics.

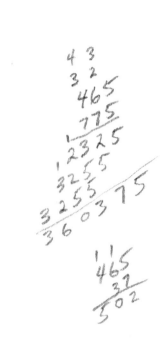

$$
\begin{array}{r}
4\ 3 \\
3\ 2 \\
4\,6\,5 \\
7\,7\,5 \\
\hline
1\ 2\,3\,2\,5 \\
3\,2\,5\,5 \\
3\,2\,5\,5 \\
\hline
3\ 6\ 0\ 3\,7\,5
\end{array}
$$

$$
\begin{array}{r}
1\ 1 \\
4\,6\,5 \\
3\,7 \\
\hline
3\,0\,2
\end{array}
$$